PORTFOLIO

UPWORLDLY MOBILE

Ranjini Manian is founder–CEO of Global Adjustments, India's premier relocation, realty and cross-cultural services company. She has had clients from seventy-five nationalities over sixteen years and has lived, worked and travelled in dozens of countries.

A multicultural expert, Ranjini pioneered India's first free cultural magazine for expatriates, *Culturama*, and is the architect of the cross-cultural e-learning portal www.globalindian.com. She has authored *Doing Business in India for Dummies*, and is a sought-after speaker. She served on the Women's Leadership Board at Harvard University.

Ranjini was schooled at Elphinstone College, Mumbai, and the University of Sorbonne, Paris. She lives in Chennai, India, with her husband and two children and responds to globalindian@globaladjustments.com.

Dear Robert,
To a lover of India, on your birthday, with great respect!
Ranjini
Dec 2, 2011

PRAISE FOR THE BOOK

'In today's globalized world, success requires understanding the nuances of other cultures. Never before in the history of the world has this been as important. Ranjini's book *Upworldly Mobile* is a great instrument for becoming a Global Indian.'

—N.R. Narayana Murthy, founder, Infosys

'Every Indian should have access to the training required to work in a multi-cultural environment. An Indian who has developed a global mindset in addition to his competencies becomes globally competitive, and culturally sensitive . . . a true professional the rest of us can rely on. *Upworldly Mobile*, in an anecdotal and practical form, addresses this very well.'

—Lakshmi Narayanan, vice-chairman, Cognizant

'Ranjini Manian's *Doing Business in India for Dummies* delivers practical advice in a fun way. Her latest, *Upworldly Mobile*, continues this trend and is a must-read for all those looking to build the behavioural skills necessary to interact globally!'

—Marshall Goldsmith, author of New York Times bestsellers *Mojo* and *What Got You Here Won't Get You There*

Upworldly Mobile

Behaviour and Business Skills for the New Indian Manager

RANJINI MANIAN

Foreword by

SHASHI THAROOR

PORTFOLIO
PENGUIN

PORTFOLIO
Published by the Penguin Group
Penguin Books India Pvt. Ltd, 11 Community Centre, Panchsheel Park, New Delhi 110 017, India
Penguin Group (USA) Inc., 375 Hudson Street, New York, New York 10014, USA
Penguin Group (Canada), 90 Eglinton Avenue East, Suite 700, Toronto, Ontario, M4P 2Y3, Canada (a division of Pearson Penguin Canada Inc.)
Penguin Books Ltd, 80 Strand, London WC2R 0RL, England
Penguin Ireland, 25 St Stephen's Green, Dublin 2, Ireland (a division of Penguin Books Ltd)
Penguin Group (Australia), 250 Camberwell Road, Camberwell, Victoria 3124, Australia (a division of Pearson Australia Group Pty Ltd)
Penguin Group (NZ), 67 Apollo Drive, Rosedale, Auckland 0632, New Zealand (a division of Pearson New Zealand Ltd)
Penguin Group (South Africa) (Pty) Ltd, 24 Sturdee Avenue, Rosebank, Johannesburg 2196, South Africa

Penguin Books Ltd, Registered Offices: 80 Strand, London WC2R 0RL, England

First published in Portfolio by Penguin Books India 2011

10 9 8 7 6 5 4 3 2 1

ISBN 9780143068037

For sale in India, Pakistan, Bangladesh, Nepal, Sri Lanka and Singapore only

Typeset in Sabon by Guru Typograph Technology, New Delhi
Printed at Gopsons Papers Ltd, Noida

With love and gratitude to my parents, Rukmani and Ramani, who strengthened my Indian roots, and yet encouraged me to fly on global wings.

WE AND THEY

Father, Mother, and Me
Sister and Auntie say
All the people like us are We,
And every one else is They.
And They live over the sea,
While We live over the way,
But—would you believe it?—
    They look upon We
As only a sort of They!

We eat pork and beef
With cow-horn-handled knives.
They who gobble Their rice
    off a leaf,
Are horrified out of Their lives;
And They who live up a tree,
And feast on grubs and clay,
(Isn't it scandalous?) look
    upon We
As a simply disgusting They!

We shoot birds with a gun.
They stick lions with spears.
Their full-dress is un-.
We dress up to Our ears.
They like Their friends for tea.
We like Our friends to stay;
And, after all that, They look
    upon We
As an utterly ignorant They!

We eat kitcheny food.
We have doors that latch.
They drink milk or blood,
Under an open thatch.
We have Doctors to fee.
They have Wizards to pay.
And (impudent heathen!) They
    look upon We
As a quite impossible They!

All good people agree,
And all good people say,
All nice people, like Us, are We
And every one else is They:
But if you cross over the sea,
Instead of over the way,
You may end by (think of it!)
    looking on We
As only a sort of They !

—Rudyard Kipling

CONTENTS

FOREWORD

A plethora of anecdotes abounds on cultural gaffes, some not so serious but some serious enough to cause loss of face. Once some US and British negotiators found themselves at a standstill when the American company proposed that they 'table' particular key points. In the US, 'tabling a motion' means not to discuss it, while the same phrase in Great Britain means to 'bring it to the table for discussion'. The food giant Kellogg had to rename its Bran Buds cereal in Sweden when it discovered that the name roughly translated to 'burned farmer'. When the soft drink company Pepsico advertised Pepsi in Taiwan with the ad 'Come Alive With Pepsi', they had no idea that it would be translated into Chinese as 'Pepsi brings your ancestors back from the dead'. A United Nations official who used the idiomatic expression 'the spirit is willing but the flesh is weak' found himself translated into Russian as saying 'the vodka is good but the meat is rotten'.

Three decades with the UN has allowed me an insight into the importance of cross-cultural understanding and the absolute necessity of sensitivity to cultural difference, whether in language, custom or modes of behaviour.

To the younger people reading this book today, let me say that you are likely to spend a lot of your professional lives interacting with people who don't look, sound, dress or eat like you; that you might work for an internationally oriented company with clients, colleagues or investors from around the globe; and that you are likely to take your holidays in far-flung destinations. To understand your clients and colleagues from across many borders and to learn to deal with such obvious albeit superficial differences, let me assure you that you do not have to look much further than this book.

Ranjini Manian has used her own experience of interactions across cultures as she has worked with foreign direct investment coming to India, while running Global Adjustments. Her book is written in an anecdotal style, replete with tales, and her simple examples are easy to absorb. This book on behavioural and business skills comes at a time when India needs to do all it can to bridge the gap between talent and its effective use. The tips in this book will be excellent tools if practised and assimilated by young professionals. The guidance it provides will also be useful for our business schools to culturally sensitize their young MBAs in order to better prepare them for the real world of global interactions.

The world's eyes are on India—on its huge market, its economic boom and its increasingly youthful population. All of us here have a growing stake in international developments. To put it another way the food we grow and eat, the air we breathe, and our health, security, prosperity and quality of life are increasingly affected by what happens beyond our borders. And that means we can simply no longer afford to be indifferent about other nations—be it our neighbours, our business partners or our trade partners. Ignorance is not a shield; in the Google age, it is not even, any longer, an excuse. Knowledge of others, on the other hand, brings great advantages in today's world. What better way to bridge this gap than to learn about each other's culture?

Upworldly Mobile takes you back to the basics. From tips on meeting and greeting, polite niceties, dress codes and addressing various people to the world of emails and conference calls and networking; from drinking alcohol at social gatherings to developing a taste for global cuisine, Ranjini has truly covered all the knowledge you might need to develop your self-confidence while dealing with colleagues of various nationalities. Anecdotes abound to make this learning process an enjoyable journey. For example, Ranjini's own experiences with her name being pronounced at Starbucks in the US will compel us all to think of how we can shorten or simplify our often complex names for our business colleagues abroad. Her interesting explanation of Lord Ganesh's photo, when asked by an American about its significance, should make us all wonder how much of our own culture we actually know, and how much we need to learn and be able to convey to others. A heartwarming letter by President Obama to his campaign supporters is printed to stress on the importance of a personal touch in furthering relationships. Individual tips on various countries are provided too: the importance of saving face in Korea, wearing the Chinese people's lucky colour (red) for a first meeting, slowing down one's speech for the Japanese and many more provide both a personal reflection of the author's past interactions and also a blueprint for the readers' future contacts.

The book allows us to believe that we can be firmly Indian in our roots and yet very global and modern in our outlook. It gives the young Indian plenty of room for negotiating his or her identity and placing it in a confident and positive category for sound interactions at the global workplace. Short tips to expatriates are provided too for a mutual cultural understanding.

It is in India's interest to ensure that the world as a whole must reflect the idea that is already familiar to all Indians—that it shouldn't matter what the colour of your skin is, the kind of food you eat, the sounds you make when you speak, the God you choose to worship (or not), so long as you want to play by the same rules as everybody else, and dream the same dreams.

We are today one of the world's largest economies, a proud player on the global stage with a long record of responsible conduct on international matters. But is our society as a whole imbued with a consciousness of the strategic opportunity that engagement with the globe offers? Can we be taken seriously as a potential world leader in the twenty-first century if we do not develop the institutions, the practices, the personnel and the mindset required to lead in the global arena?

This book offers a useful contribution to changing our collective mindsets. I commend it particularly to the young people of India who must shape the future orientation of this country to the world. You are a new, globalized, impatient generation of Indians who rightly refuse to be confined to the limited worldviews of older generations. The horizons of your world are ever widening. The prospects for international engagement, for more widespread prosperity, for more borderless success, have never been brighter. But the world needs your commitment too.

I call upon you all today to commit yourself to thinking about India and the world—about India in the world—and your own role in learning about it, helping to shape it and one day, I hope, helping to lead it. Ranjini Manian's book *Upworldly Mobile* will, without doubt, guide you to being successful professionals, making yourselves proud and making your country prouder.

All the best.

Dr Shashi Tharoor, M.P.

AUTHOR'S NOTE

'It's the details that make the difference between the mediocre and the magnificent' read a poster in an office I once visited. The accompanying illustration was a close-up of a peacock's tail, spread out in all its many-hued splendour. Successfully doing business in India, or anywhere else in the world for that matter, is a lot about getting the details right.

There is only one thing better than being an Indian . . . it is being an Indian in the twenty-first century . . . and that too an Indian representing his/her trade in the world in the twenty-first century. As two-way traffic between India and the world is in full swing in this period of post-liberalization, I realize that this is the time to drop our timidity; it is time to step out into the world. Global recognition awaits any Indian business, small or large, that excels.

Experience has taught me that to excel the management cadre needs to be aware of details that are often overlooked in the push to master trade strategies and acquire business acumen. Simultaneously something Robert Kohls, father of cross-cultural studies and founder of the Society of Intercultural Education and Research (SIETAR), once said to me echoes in my mind: 'Preserve your Indian roots, and take global wings. The total westernization of India is the worst thing that could happen.'

My company, Global Adjustments, which offers focused integrated cross-cultural and destination services for expatriates and Indians, maintaining the highest standards of professionalism and integrity, is powered by the vision of creating empowered global citizens through real life solutions, leveraging the India expertise.

We promote it through our workshops, coaching and branding events where India takes centre stage and becomes a shining beacon for the world to follow in adaptation to cultural diversity. In the course of our sixteen years of experience beginning 1995, easing passages to and from India, we've acquired a great deal of collective wisdom interacting with seventy-five nationalities who moved to India to do business, which I've been privileged to share via mentoring articles for the New Manager in *Business Line*, the premier business daily from the *Hindu* group of Newspapers. This book has its seed in those articles. From cellphone etiquette to cultural mindsets, handshaking to handing in things on time, from cuisines to conversation starters, they're all here.

It is my hope that this book will open the windows of the new Indian Manager's mind to what the Thomas Friedman-flattened business world expects as a 'common minimum platform', to borrow a phrase from the politician's lexicon. Our former prime minister, the late Indira Gandhi, once said: 'If you wish to know something about India, you must empty your mind of all preconceived notions. Why be imprisoned by the limited vision of the prejudiced? Don't try to compare. India is different and, exasperating as it may seem, would like to remain so . . .' That being so, I have included special pull-outs for the benefit of expatriate managers in the book. I hope these will help chart a road map to the Indian businessman's soul.

If my team and I can hold on to Indian roots and yet fly comfortably high with all global interactions, then anyone can. And the best news is, you don't have to give up being who you are; you simply adapt knowing you will be more successful. Don't say 'let them adapt'; remember the time is advantage India. Why not ace them? Global Indians, there is only one way to go—UP.

So, here's to the new, magnificent manager!

PART 1

Building Bridges

> 'As human beings, our greatness lies not so much in being able to remake the world . . . as in being able to remake ourselves.'
>
> —Mahatma Gandhi

The very first step to knowing another culture is knowing one's own. The art is in knowing why we do what we do, and what drives us from the depths of our value system and manifests above the watermark of the cultural iceberg. Once we live in self-awareness and start developing responses, we are well on our way to the next step which is to adapt to another culture.

We need to be aware, for instance, that Indian names are long and we tend to rattle them off rather fast as that is our way of being self-effacing, that our handshakes are weak because we see it as a sign of respect not to push ourselves forward with senior people, that we drop in unannounced as we value relationship building and don't think of privacy first, and that we are uncomfortable with smiling and eye contact as we fear we could be termed too 'forward'. Only if we know these things can we even make any attempt to change ourselves or help the world adapt to us.

This section looks at making ourselves self-aware and provides tips to implement changes for successfully becoming a Global Indian.

1

HOW TO MEET AND GREET

What's in a Name?

Indian names can prove difficult for a foreigner to pronounce. Without westernizing our names or losing our own culture, how can we find the middle path? Chuck ego out the door, and look for ease of understanding.

Recently in the US when I ordered coffee at Starbucks, a chain of popular coffee shops, they asked me for my name. I said 'Ranjini' but the person at the counter had to ask me two or three times before being able to take down my name, and I could feel those behind me in the queue grow restless. The Starbucks staff did, however, need to get my name to call it out when the order of coffee was ready. This happened twice. By the third time, I found a way out. I gave my name as 'Jini': just two syllables and, moreover, a name that didn't sound so different from the Western 'Ginny'. The understanding has been instantaneous and the experience, spot on since then.

This reminded me of a recent news article I read. Pradyumna Thiruvenkatanathan had won a Cambridge MIT scholarship. How, I wondered, would Pradyumna be getting on with his name? Would he be at all addressed by his seven-syllabled last name—Thi-ru-ven-ka-ta-na-than? If I had known him, I would love to have asked.

Students from Chennai are attending Nobel laureate seminars. Indian professionals from New Delhi are attending conferences the world over. Direct-to-home television companies are telemarketing from Mumbai to the US all the time. Indians and the world are fully connected. So what can we do to get over the name stumbling block?

WHAT'S YOUR GOOD NAME?

In the Hindu tradition, when naming a baby, one of the Sanskrit mantras says: 'Your name is "Brahman" ("the one true self in all").' Then, for transaction purposes, another one is given. Often we choose a god's name to call the child so that each time the name is uttered, spiritual merit is also collected and the vibrations are good. When a mother on her deathbed calls out for her daughter or son, she is also calling the Lord's name. All this thought has gone into the Hindu naming tradition.

Fast-forward to the twenty-first century when India is becoming a superpower because of our knowledge of the English language. Besides, we are good with digits, and Indians are much sought after for both. For transacting with this global village that we call our world, our multi-syllabled names are posing challenges. Without westernizing our names or losing our own culture how can we find the middle path? Chuck ego out the door, and look for ease of understanding. Go with some comfort level to please yourself but also put the other person first.

It isn't as if we lose our cultural identity as some cultures may feel they do by adopting completely Western names. The Starbucks person, for instance, or even someone I work with on a project is not someone I live or work with and shortening my name for transactions only makes the job easier.

NOT MORE THAN TWO SYLLABLES

We have to find a comfortable, shortened version of our name—one we can live with. If it is one-syllabled it will be easy to register—Raj is easier than Gopal for Rajgopal—but to try and restrict it to no more than two syllables is most effective.

CONSONANTS APART

Most other languages find it hard to handle sounds that have two consonants without a vowel in between. For instance, 'mn' in 'Pradyumna', the hero of our earlier story who went to MIT, is hard for most others. The Indian tongue can twist and turn easier than others, shall we say? In such cases, it is best to find a short name which simplifies this process. Don't ask me why but a friend I met in Silicon Valley is called Rocky instead of Satish!

INITIALS ARE A BREEZE

One easy way out is to say 'I am Jayakrishna Bhatt; please call me J.K. for short.' In India, we get used to initials easily and people from overseas find it easy to remember and say them too. So this is a good via media to go with.

PRONUNCIATIONS AND MEANINGS HELP

It is perfectly OK to take the time to help others get the pronunciation right using some mnemonic device: 'My name is Ram; it is pronounced like CD-ROM, not the animal ram.' Chances are the other person will get it right away. Find out what your name means and help others remember by telling them the meaning. It is appreciated if you say 'Ravi means sun, or Chandra means moon.'

Insight for Outsiders:

Just break it up!

One of my expatriate clients surprised me with his deeply intuitive understanding of the Indian naming game. He said, 'I have understood now that most of your names are a string of different gods' names, for example, Siva-rama-krishna or Uma-mahesh or Sita-ram.' That makes it easier on the memory, doesn't it?

Our names don't fit in a form when we travel and they go way off the space provided in the passport too. Initials sometimes confuse by standing after our names. Let's clearly work out and have a first name–last name system in our own minds as computers in Western universities accept this data as the first capture before all else. Most computer codes are written in India or by Indians anyway, so why lose out with our names? We have a lot more going for us.

Tackling Honorifics and Other Titles

Cues to beginning a professional relationship correctly

What may I call you, please? Asking this question, listening to the response to it and then following the instruction given is the most candid and important way to break the ice and build a sustainable relationship when meeting someone for the first time.

I met a couple of US congressmen the other day at a dinner party in India. That was the first time I was meeting a congressman (the equivalent of our member of Parliament, I found out). I was introduced to Sheila Jackson Lee, and I asked, 'May I call you Sheila?' Her response, in a polite, instantly familiar American tone, was: 'Sure, whatever name is easy for you to retain.' But I later found others in the congressional party calling her 'Congresswoman Jackson Lee' and the other person, 'Congressman Moran'. So I followed suit and thus stuck to protocol.

DON'T DROP THAT TITLE

The title of a dignitary must be maintained, so it's better to get it right the first time; but otherwise at least listen, learn and imitate. Titles are precious to those on whom they have been conferred.

A medical degree or a doctorate is usually earned after much hard work; so in using the title 'Dr' while addressing a medical practitioner or a PhD holder, you are showing respect for the person's educational qualifications. You can't go wrong there. And while addressing top diplomats and the heads of missions, it is customary to use titles like 'Ambassador' and 'Your Excellency', as appropriate.

MR, MRS YA MS?

But what about the common 'Mr', 'Mrs' and 'Miss'? Sometimes, their use can be tricky. For instance, at times you may be unsure whether it is a man or a woman you are addressing in an email—the name could belong to either sex—like the English name Ashley or the Indian names Roop and Kiran. When in doubt, use the full name leaving out titles; say 'Dear Ashley Philips' or 'Roop Chander' or 'Kiran Kapoor', as the case may be. And if you have to send a letter to someone you know is a woman, fall back on the tried and trusted 'Ms' (pronounced 'miz'). 'Ms' is a neutral alternative that doesn't concern itself with a woman's marital status.

These tips are mainly for written communications and formal meetings. They need not be observed on all occasions when you meet the same people, especially once you establish a degree of comfort with them and they request you to drop the formality.

Many Westerners wonder why Indians can't simply address them the way they want to be addressed.

Insight for Outsiders:

Calling names

The honorific 'Sir' has regional translations like 'Saab' in Hindi, 'Ayya' in Tamil, 'Saheb' in Marathi. It is hard for

Indian professionals to call expatriates by their first name at the workplace. In traditional India, sons-in-law and daughters-in-law don't even use the names of their parents-in-law within their earshot.

HIRE OR HIERARCHY?

During my visit to a joint venture company to facilitate a team building multicultural workshop, an executive assistant to the co-CEOs said in front of her two bosses, 'I am confused; Tom Hawkins wants me to call him Tom and I know Sanjay Prafulla wants me to call him Sir; so which one do I have to follow?' This is because in India, in traditional corporate interaction, seniors like to be called 'Sir' or addressed as 'Mr so-and-so'. In the US 'Sir' is used mainly for the military while in the UK, it could refer to the high honour of a knighthood in which case the person is addressed by his first name prefixed with 'Sir'.

We Indians are taught from early childhood that it is disrespectful to address grown-ups by their given names. We carry these instructions through into adulthood and, even when specifically asked to drop the 'Mr', 'Sir' or 'Ma'am', persist in using these titles. Actually, we could end up annoying Westerners in the process. Recently, Brian Woolworth from Wales was in a 'working in India' programme I ran. He said he found it difficult to handle so much 'Sir-ing'. He also asked when his team of eighty engineers would stop jumping up and quickly tidying their desks if he came around for a chat. The trick is for us to always have our desks more or less organized, so we would be confident both when the boss is there and not there.

Also pause to think for a minute—is your refusal to adopt the less formal form of address a matter of your personal comfort? If the other person is not comfortable with your mode of address, wouldn't it be better to put his or her comfort before your own?

MAKING PEACE WITH THEIR PIECE

I also told Brian not to have too many informal chats till his team felt at ease with him and also to talk to them over a coffee about his work and personal interaction style. After all, good manners have to be about feeling at ease both ways; so we do teach Westerners to adapt too, and believe me they are willing.

When I met Jeff Bezos of Amazon.com, he said, 'Call me Jeff.' I found that everyone in his entourage called him 'Jeff', so I followed suit and built that relationship. While writing to him I kept it formal but while speaking I used his first name. On the other hand when I first met Captain Shantanu Banerjee, I asked him my favourite question, 'What may I call you, please?' The response was 'Whatever you like,' but knowing he had come from a navy background and was now a corporate leader in a multinational job, I used the title 'Captain' when I continued with my dialogue. My presentation went rather well because of that, I thought.

Insight for Outsiders:

Seen and (not) heard

In India, it is common to presume that a woman is the non-working partner. Indians are quite capable of looking through a woman in a small circle of people in conversation, as they have learnt to tune out and take for granted the man as the breadwinner in the circle. International women are requested not to take this as a personal insult but simply a stereotype that has formed in the Indian mind. It is quite OK to gently remind onlookers to include you as a woman in the conversation or to even say directly, 'Actually we are in India because of my job and I would like to participate in this conversation.' Indians will quickly correct the error and will turn to you respectfully, albeit a bit taken aback.

So remember, be a chameleon and switch as the occasion demands.

Your Dress Sense Speaks Volumes

You are what you wear, at least in the beholder's eyes.

How many times have we agonized over the question, 'What shall I wear?' The question becomes even more confusing if you happen to live in a place that is culturally distinct from your own with a totally different dressing style. Many of us these days travel abroad on work. Then the question acquires even greater importance: 'What do I wear to work?'

There is the obvious factor of the weather. While cotton shirts and trousers are the norm in India, in colder climates a jacket is a must. But apart from this, my advice would be to blend in with the locals and choose muted colours instead of that green shirt you might pick back home.

FORMAL VERSUS CASUAL

Make sure your accessories match your outfit and the occasion, and that you're well groomed.

Men, carry a 'bandh gala' Nehru suit as it is a much-admired outfit, though a well-tailored, double-breasted suit is also a must. Ensure your clothes are of good quality lest they rip at the most inopportune moments.

Women, carry a stole that can be slung over your shoulder; this East meets West dressing style is elegant and would make you feel secure too. If a dot on the forehead is a must, then by all means sport it with Indian clothes or Western wear but be ready to answer why you do so—that it is the third eye of knowledge, reminding you to look inward. And ladies, tone down your make-up—no overly kohl-rimmed eyes and bright lipsticks to the office. You would feel too dressed up!

For shopping or sightseeing, the thumb rule is wear what you're comfortable in—jeans, T-shirts, skirts and even shorts. Remember, the West is far more liberal in dress style than the Orient. But take care not to attract unwanted attention. If you're invited to a wedding abroad, it would be all right to wear an Indian outfit but make sure it isn't over the top in terms of both embellishments and accessories.

Besides being appropriately dressed, do give a thought to your own comfort. For instance, if you have a whole-day meeting, don't wear something that is tight and is likely to make you uncomfortable. And if the air conditioning is likely to be going full blast, dress accordingly.

Insight for Outsiders:

When in India . . .

On the other side of the coin, expats need to be aware that standards of dressing in India are different from those in the West. While sightseeing, remember to carry a scarf; some temples require you to cover your hair. Shoes that are easy to put on and take off are a must if you are attending a religious ceremony.

Whether it's India or abroad, the saying 'Clothes maketh the man' is valid. You are often judged by what you wear, particularly if you need to interact with bureaucracy. I remember waiting at a local administrative office for a certificate. The place was teeming with people from all walks of life. Apparently, no one there had heard of the queue system with people clamouring to be heard and officials acting like they were in noise-proof bubbles. Then in walked a lady, very well turned out in a silk sari, wearing matching jewellery and tasteful make-up. The crowds parted for her like magic. She was treated with the utmost deference by everyone, and doors which had remained stubbornly closed earlier opened eagerly.

Like the others there I thought she was a VIP, and spent some time fruitlessly trying to place her. When finally I got a chance to enter the concerned official's room, I found her seated inside while a peon sorted through files to find what she needed. She started a conversation with me, and I asked her about herself. It turned out she was an advocate and had come to collect some certificates for a client. I'm sure there were other advocates there on similar missions but her way of dressing ensured priority treatment. If you dress well, you get treated well.

Remember, at times, 'less is more'—understated clothes set off by classy accessories can speak volumes. And wear a smile; it is your best accessory.

Insight for Outsiders:

SMILE—it's what makes the world go round!

Indians are said to be a more serious race. In countries that smile the most, India came one-hundred-and-twenty-third! Denmark was placed at Number One as the happiest and most-smiling nation of the world. Don't be surprised though if the opposite is true and you find many on the street who just have a shirt on their back and yet seem happy!

Breaking the Ice

It's hard to make that first contact, to establish those good vibes. But it is simple if you know how it works.

I was in a cashier's queue at a lifestyle store. An expatriate was standing ahead of me. Since my company's business is to welcome expatriates, I would have loved to make contact but I didn't want to appear pushy. I wondered how to draw her attention.

While I waited in line, I listened as she spoke to the cashier. Her accent sounded French. She happened to be buying a bowl that was chipped and I used the French I knew to point out the flaw. Earlier in the queue though, I had already made eye contact and smiled. She thanked me and then I asked her if by any chance Renault had brought her to India, using information that I had read in recent news reports. 'What else?' she quipped. We became friends and she is now a client.

SEIZE THE MOMENT!

On the other hand, my colleague told me that she was in the lobby of a five-star hotel and her attempt to make connections failed. An expatriate was seated in a chair close by, reading. My colleague, wanting to bring in some business, walked up to him and introduced herself. 'But he just brushed me aside,' said my colleague, crestfallen. 'How would you have handled the opportunity?'

Well, it's all about breaking the ice. If you don't do it subtly, you just might find yourself in a freezing lake! Breaking the ice is an art, not only in a business context but also in a social one. In either a business or a social situation, coming on too strong is bound to put off your prospective contact. Even a straightforward introduction, putting you in a business context, is likely to be seen as propositioning for a sale and may not be appreciated.

SLOW AND CONFIDENT

Say something sincerely complimentary about the person you're trying to get to know and make eye contact with a smile.

At a 1600-attendee international conference in Los Angles, US, I was impressed with the keynote speaker. (It is always a great idea to sit up front at such events and on an aisle seat for ease of jumping up and meeting the key people right after they speak.) I went right up to him, gave him a firm handshake, smiled and told him what specific part of his talk I found useful. The next thing I knew he had invited me to attend his $3000 executive education programme free. He was none other than Marshall Goldsmith, author of the best-seller *What Got You Here Won't Get You There*, now America's top executive coach. Today, Marshall has turned into a mentor, has visited us in India and even coached my team!

To make initial contact, it'll be good if you find something in common with the person. For this, you need to be both observant and well-informed. And give a sincere specific compliment.

PREPARATION

Make it your business to know some facts—historical, current, archaeological, cultural or social. I never take a meeting without running an Internet search on the company or the person. The information can make for useful conversation openers.

To get back to the man in the hotel lobby, my colleague told me he had been reading a book. I would probably have used that as my starting point. If I had read the book myself, I would have commented on it or another by the same author. Failing that, I would have taken out a copy of our in-house magazine, flipped through it and offered it to him saying it had some interesting inputs for expatriates.

That brings me to another important factor. Be prepared with an interesting icebreaker tool. When I travel on international flights I always carry a few ten-rupee notes which show fifteen of our Indian languages. Have something similar to do so that you can use it as a follow-up after breaking the ice.

BE HELPFUL

Another good beginning would be to help. It automatically shows you in a favourable light. Drawing attention to the damaged bowl she was buying helped start my relationship with the lady from Renault and it wouldn't have mattered if I had only been able to do it in English and she was more comfortable in French.

Be natural, be yourself, smile and make eye contact because these things are the most important elements in any relationship. 'Relationship' is the key word here.

The lady at the lifestyle store became my friend before she became my client. It is important to establish a relationship with the person first. Business will most probably follow but in any case you will gain from the personal interaction. If the man in the hotel had shown an interest in our in-house magazine, I would have gone on to explain what my company does and would have invited him over to see our facilities. Even if he didn't show any inclination to start a conversation, I would have told him that if he needed further information on anything that the magazine talked about, he had only to use the email helpline in it. I would then have introduced myself to the manager at the hotel's reception and offered our complimentary help with city or cultural information if he needed it for expatriates staying in the hotel, just to assist him in his job.

Follow-up is important. After our meeting at the lifestyle store, I sent my new friend a little note and some information on our city. She had scribbled her cellphone number for me, which I used only after impressing her with a note. I invited her to the office, she accepted, and our mutually satisfactory association was on its way. So here are the steps:

- See the world as good.
- See yourself as likeable.
- Smile; make eye contact.

- Don't come on strong; get comfortable first.
- Don't sell, if that is what you want to do.
- Ask for advice and the sale automatically follows.

Let's Shake on It

Simple gestures can firm up a business relationship.

The first time at anything is 'butterflies in the stomach' time for most of us. We tend to shy away from the unknown and even the most confident among us will surely wonder, at least in passing, if we are following proper etiquette (yes, it is pronounced 'eh-ticket' even in the plural, or worry about committing a faux pas (and yes, that is pronounced 'fo pa').

At a business meeting, particularly one involving expatriates, the butterflies could well multiply. You're assailed by a million doubts—'How should I shake hands? Just a fleeting touch? Take a firm grip? Hold the guest's hand between both of my own? After I receive the foreign guests, do I step aside for them to go through the doors first? Or do I precede them?' Let's look at a few answers to these unending questions.

SHAKING HANDS

Let's take handshakes first since that is a must-do when greeting expatriates and something that doesn't come naturally to us Indians. The right and only way to shake the hand of a person you're meeting for the first time is to hold firm and shake briefly, just long enough for both to say your names. Take care not to squeeze the other person's hand but don't let your hand hang limp either. The introductory handshake is one of the ways in which first impressions are created. A firm handshake, web to web, conveys confidence, interest and respect. A cupped handshake or the 'glove', where your left hand covers the normal handshake, is unusual and reserved for politicians or condolence in some countries!

> **Insight for Outsiders:**
>
> *Take a bow.*
>
> Indians use the namaste gesture with folded palms traditionally which means 'I bow to the divine in you'. In business situations Indians will typically use the handshake though not always as firm and confident as you would like it. A soft handshake, or a 'wet rag' as you perceive it, is done out of respect to you as the visiting guest. Don't perceive it as a weakness in character. Don't offer a namaste in a business situation either as it could be insulting that you think we don't know how to greet businesslike. Do use the namaste for older folks socially though; it will be much appreciated that you learned.
>
> Limp handshakes are a way of showing respect in India. Indians don't think it appropriate to show aggression when they are trying to show respect of hierarchy or for authority, so they offer a soft handshake to show they are being respectful, blissfully unaware that this is being misconstrued as lack of 'solid character'.

OK, so you've got the handshake over. Now you need to escort your guests into the hotel and the conference hall. The swinging or revolving doors have to be negotiated first. See if the doorman is present to operate the door. If so, stand back and allow your guests to go through first. If not, you go ahead and help the guests come in. Usher them to the conference hall.

Networking for Impact

INTRODUCTION TO INTRODUCTIONS

Now you have to perform introductions. Whose name should

you bring up first: your boss's name or the client's? The rule of thumb is you introduce the person with the greater authority first. If your boss takes precedence in rank, then you introduce him or her first. However, a client always gets the higher position. The correct form would be to say: 'Ms Amrita Pandey, may I introduce *to you* Mr John Doe, chief marketing manager of ABC?' Go on to say, 'Mr Doe, meet Ms Pandey, our CEO.' Remember, say 'introduce *to* you' and refer to the person who has the higher rank, rather than say 'introduce *you* to'.

Whew! That's over and done with. 'Now, let me get myself something to drink,' you tell yourself. 'A beer would calm me down.' You catch the nearest waiter's eye and pick up a frosty glass from the tray and begin to mingle. After all, you're still on duty and there are lots of people you need to meet or renew contact with: all the more reason to make sure you don't go beyond one alcoholic drink.

You wander around, drink in hand, when someone comes up with an outstretched hand. Oh, oh! What do you do with your drink? Transfer it from your right hand to your left. But your right hand is damp from the condensation on the glass; you're stuck with offering a wet handshake. Oops! It's sensible to hold your drink in your left hand, so that your right one can be free for a handshake at any time, and a dry one at that! On its way up, your open palm could be subtly but firmly brushed against your clothes to ensure dryness too.

You don't drink alcohol, you say. Many in India and even across the world, I realize, don't. At Global Adjustments, we have relocated to India chairmen and CEOs of Fortune 500 companies who are teetotallers! But at business meets, where there's usually a cocktail and networking hour, it is considered polite to have some sort of a drink in hand (juice, soda or even mineral water). You'll need to raise your glass (shoulder level is the right height to raise it to, not all the way to the ceiling in your enthusiasm) if someone proposes a toast. Also, it's useful to be able to take a sip from time to time while you look around and decide what you have to do next.

IS COURTESY DEAD?

I recall a relocation conference I attended in Denver in the US where there were *over* 1000 international people present. It was a luncheon meet and during the networking hour, we were invited to sit down at a beautifully laid table so that business conversations could continue over the meal. One of the senior leaders from a visiting company was a lady. I watched as a man from the host firm, who was walking with her, politely drew out a chair and invited her to sit. 'Would you believe it?' the lady in question said, turning a beaming face to me after she had thanked the official, 'Courtesy isn't dead yet!'

Gestures like proper handshakes, confident introductions, opening doors and pulling out chairs are taken as signs of courtesy universally. Believe me, they ease the path of the most difficult business deals and send your stock up a million points at networking events.

2

IT'S JUST ONE WORLD AFTER ALL

Touching Base with Culture

It's always nice to be well informed about our own traditions and customs.

I was once in the sunny region of San Francisco in mid-April. As I flew in there on the eve of Baisakhi and the Tamil New Year, India was on my mind and also in the imagination of Americans.

Union Square, in the heart of San Francisco, has a lovely multi-storeyed shoppers' paradise called Macy's. Looming large on the facade of Macy's was a 20-foot statue of Ganesh and a large attractive poster in fuchsia and orange shouting out 'Imagine India'. The thousands of tourists taking streetcar (tram) rides, the passers-by listening to live music on Union Square, the shoppers, the businessmen—all catch a glimpse of Ganesh. Excitedly I took out my camera to document, yet again, India's far and wide reach in today's world.

WHO MOVED MY MODAK?

A businessman in a suit hurriedly walked past me and then suddenly retraced his steps. 'I have been wanting to know: why is there a rat at the bottom with a piece of cheese?' he asked me. Caught off guard only momentarily, I engaged my captive victim with age-old Indian wisdom! 'First the cheese is poetic licence by the Western artist who built this statue; an Indian depiction would be holding a sweet called 'modak'. Second, the rat stands for desire. The idea is that it is perfectly OK to have legitimate desires, so long as we are their masters. That is why desire is depicted as a small, lively creature going about its business at the feet of Ganesh who is lording over it.' He seemed to love that one-minute explanation as I heard many American sounds: 'Wow, cool . . . what an awesome idea!' and he walked on to, no doubt, the next appointment on his schedule.

This incident made me think how important it is for us to be able to understand and explain our own culture. The truth is most of what we experience—traditions and rituals, values and beliefs—has just been imbibed and taken for granted. It is not easy for us to put things succinctly into words so that other people can understand the essence in simple terms, unless we consciously learn to do so.

- *Self-confidence comes from knowledge*: When we know the whys and wherefores behind things, we develop a sense of pride and confidence in ourselves and our culture. We understand the rationale behind rituals and can explain them. It makes our cultural foundation strong.
- *Knowledge aids communication*: Once this knowledge is thorough and clear, we can logically present it to the outside world so any layperson can understand us. We know what we know and we also know how to say this. The two steps of knowledge and communication are equally important.
- *Communication builds relationships*: Once we communicate logically and with clarity, it makes for a sense of renewed respect in the eyes of the listener and we are taken seriously. The relationship is strong when based on sound knowledge and clear communication.

The three steps above are important in all relationships—business or social. In intercultural relations, it is extremely important to know your own culture, for this acts as a bridge towards understanding others. This forms the basis of effective teams and multicultural success as we interact in a flattened world.

Insight for Outsiders:

We have the same differences.

Back in the US, I faced the next question of the week: 'So tell us about castes in India. Do people of all castes frequent the same bars? How should I, as a foreigner, be treating differences?'

I stifled a laugh at the image this evoked and explained it all in one breath: 'We don't all frequent bars in India that often. But sure, if we did "hang out" in bars, which would only be in urban India, we wouldn't be checking castes at all.' As an expatriate, you just need to treat us all with the same respect and not take any notice of differences.

We, as Global Indians, need to know our own culture (even the difficult-to-explain parts), understand others' time and reference limitation, and be able to communicate just enough and effectively. It is the first step towards being outstanding Global Indians. As the Bhagavad Gita says, 'What the outstanding person does, others will try to do. The standards such people create will be followed by the whole world.'

Bridging Cultural Differences

All it takes to build a cross-cultural business relationship is respect and a little bit of effort.

Recently, a senior manager in our firm clinched a deal with a Dutch company to train and relocate employees of a global mobile company in India. One of the principal reasons he stuck in the mind of his company's executives was the personalized relationship that he developed with them. This relationship was not built by giving them gifts or wining and dining with them; it was through email exchanges that went like this:

> Goedemorgen Danielle!
>
> I just wanted to point out our presence through strong seamless partnerships to cover the North and South of India for your business.
>
> Raj

> Namaste Raj,
>
> That is good to hear, pls send us your best quotes.
>
> Danielle

> Dank u, Danielle!
>
> We will need till Monday to do a thorough job of presenting you our best quotes for all locations.
>
> Raj
>
> We are glad you can cover those regions in one go. We will wait for Monday next week, no problem, and with pleasure.
>
> Enjoy Kranti Divas Raj.
> Danielle

GREET IN THEIR LANGUAGE

Excuses such as not speaking a foreign language or not knowing where to go for just a few words and phrases in a foreign language are no longer valid, because your friendly neighbourhood Google is at your cyber-doorstep. 'Namaste' and 'Goedemorgen' are available at the other end of your mouse and have made a positive impact when both parties in the email exchange above opened their mailboxes!

KNOW EACH OTHER'S FESTIVE DAYS

Danielle didn't know earlier that 9 August is called Kranti Divas. Why, even many of us may not remember this name for the day which marks the anniversary of Gandhiji's launch of the Quit India Movement in 1942. But Google will prompt you any time. Again, it strikes the right chord when we greet someone of another culture with knowledge of an occasion they celebrate. For instance, 'Enjoy Columbus Day' would go down well as a closing remark in a phone call with an American, if you remember to mention it in the first week of October. (For Americans, the second Monday of October is a celebration of Christopher Columbus's discovery of America.)

USE THEIR NAME

Indians are shy about using someone's name as doing so was traditionally considered a mark of disrespect. But a person's name is the sweetest sound to him or her. So do get over this and consciously use people's names when interacting with them.

One step further—we had a German client coming to our office the other day. We usually have a client profile form and get to know about his/her family or company so that we can strike a personal chord in the first conversation. But this time we had no detail except his name: Weidman. A few minutes with Google, and we came up with the meaning of his name—'hunter'—in German. That was enough ammunition for a conversation starter that he enjoyed when we met.

'"Weidman" means hunter, doesn't it?'

(*Smiling and happy*) 'Oh yes, we in Germany use professions . . .' and so it went.

Using the other person's name during conversations, in emails or telephone calls or in face-to-face meetings works very well to build a personalized professional relationship.

Insight for Outsiders:

There's a lot in a name!

Indians traditionally didn't use each other's names as it was a mark of disrespect to call out someone's name. A husband in rural India might still call his wife 'Tunnu ki ma' (Tunnu's mom) where Tunnu is their son, and the wife would call her husband 'ji', just an honorific suffix, not his name. A younger Indian at home will never call an older one, such as a grandparent, aunt or older brother, by name. This translates from family values to national and corporate values. So don't be surprised if you don't hear Indians use your or each other's names much, and if at all they do it will be with an addition of 'Mr' or 'Ms'. When you use Indian names they will be delighted that you 'actually called' them by their name, which is a sign of being 'close' to someone. But do work on getting pronunciations right. A first name may be written 'sankar' but it is pronounced more like 'shun-ker', not 'san-ker' rhyming with 'ran'.

ASK FOR MORE TIME OR DETAILS

Asking, in a clear manner, for the time you need to do a job properly or for more details to do it thoroughly is actually a good sign. Raj, in the case above, asked for time till Monday and Danielle readily agreed. Now he can do the job well against a relaxed deadline. Let's develop the confidence to do this; all it takes is for us to start off asking, even if we are sorely tempted by conditioning to simply agree or comply.

STATE THE FACTS CONFIDENTLY

If something is true (such as Raj having six physical offices but capable of actually serving sixteen locations through them), state it confidently. There is no need to be shy, feel awkward or, worse still, to underplay or exaggerate facts.

DELIVER WHAT YOU SAY, WHEN YOU SAY YOU WILL

This is the most important part: If you promise something, then you have to keep it. If you say you will send the quote on Monday, it has to be there on Monday at 9 a.m. or at least by noon—even if there is no power, a bug got in your computer, your colleague stayed home or there was a sudden personal situation! You have to take full responsibility and deliver what you committed to by always having a 'Plan B' for such situations, which are common in our country. (In situations like those above use a cyber café, use the back-up CD that you should have been making and maintaining regularly, do the job yourself or get a colleague to do it to meet the given deadline.) Warn the other person, in exceptional cases, of further delays as soon as you know it may happen, instead of hoping to somehow get it done in time. Your credibility in globalized relationships is built on your timely and reliable delivery at the end of the day, and not on your personal standing in society.

'I speak your language—works wonders,' literally and figuratively! So good luck to Global Indians.

3

CROSSING THE CULTURAL OCEANS

The Art of Intercultural Networking

Getting to know our guests as people first can be a rewarding experience.

We were at the launch of the Mumbai edition of *Culturama*, our monthly cultural magazine which is intended to help expatriates understand India and hear their experiences in the country. The room was filled with people from various countries. We had ninety minutes to get to know each other, spread awareness of the magazine and leave a lasting impression on as many attendees as possible. On the flight back to Chennai, I made a list of all the attendees I had met and interacted with that evening. I was delighted to discover that I had interacted with people from seventeen nationalities who call India their home.

My colleague asked for tips on how to manage to meet, interact with and remember so many people. That set me thinking once again: 'If I can do it, anyone can.' So here are some methods to network across cultures.

BOOST YOUR SELF-ESTEEM

Prior to an event, and in fact starting today, remind yourself by writing down a list, if you like, of up to twenty things you are good at. It could be a skill—'I am a great cook/singer', a trait—'I am patient/caring', or a relationship—'I am a good dad/faithful friend/great team member'. The list could include—'I am a good speaker, swimmer, listener, programmer, gadget fixer and multitasker.' Most of it will apply to you and if you can't come up with twenty items to make the list, ask friends and family to help you with it. This list boosts your self esteem and, no, it won't make you arrogant!

Now be confident that people do want to meet you because you are good, and approach networking events confidently. Keep your right hand and smile ready. Proactively go up to meet each new person with an open smile and a firm handshake. Use a one-line descriptor self-introduction which comes to you easily. You should write this down beforehand and practise it, so that it does not sound contrived or unnatural: 'Hello, I am Navin (slowly) Agarwal (still slower), senior analyst from XYZ Technologies in Noida.'

ASK WITH GENUINE INTEREST

Openly ask the other guests which country they come from or what brings them to India. There is a fine line that distinguishes between asking too many questions or personal ones, and not asking any because you are shy or don't know what is appropriate. If you genuinely care and ask sincerely, it is always disarmingly simple and will win answers and friendships.

I once made the mistake of asking the question 'Are you American?' and discovered that the person was a Canadian who disliked being taken for an American. His monosyllabic response ended the conversation negatively. Instead of hazarding a guess, which is meant to show off my intelligence, I have learnt to tone down the question and simply ask, 'Which country do you come from?' Should it be 'Canada', I say 'Your accent was lovely, I couldn't exactly place it.' This helps build bridges of cultural friendship much better.

CURIOUS OR INQUISITIVE

Questions such as 'What brings you to India?' or 'What do you do in Mumbai?' are better than a more direct 'Which company do you work for?' Never give people the impression that you are sizing them up and are going to decide, based on their responses, if you want to continue to know them. Even when the response is 'My husband's work', don't ask 'Where does he work?'. Instead, use 'What field is he in?' That is a good lead into conversations—non-threatening and perfectly acceptable.

LISTEN AND TAKE MENTAL NOTES

Always talk in the other person's interest. Asking Sakura-san—the head of a Japanese auto manufacturer—how he manages for Japanese food in India and how much you enjoy eating 'tempura', which are like Indian 'bajjis' or Udon Noodles, is sure to whet his appetite to continue the conversation. Just being a good listener makes them want to be in touch and can even lead to an exchange of business cards, which is the goal of networking. After the event, as soon as possible, make notes on who you met, what you learnt about them and draw up a follow-up action plan. Following through with a brief 'thank you' email could lead to positive outcomes in business and social relationships.

With the world shrinking, many of us may have to engage in multicultural tête-à-têtes.

Meet Me Halfway, Please

It's all a matter of give and take.

Let me start with a real-life story which we hear rather regularly in managing expatriate expectation. After a month of settling into a new home had extended to two months of finishing touches and after much back and forth on details, there were some strained relations between a Western tenant and his Indian realtor. The Westerner was fed up, culture shocked, removed from the familiar and planted into a new space which was frustrating. The realtor had no control over the last 20 per cent of the home finish, which seemed to take 80 per cent of the time; all she had to offer was constant follow-up and her goodwill.

Andreas (*unsmiling, towering at six feet four inches, blonde and blue-eyed*): Yes?

Lakshmi (*smiling and cheerful, dressed in a lovely sari*): Good evening, Andreas. I came by as I couldn't reach you on the phone. I just wanted to see if you were settling in OK, as I know you had teething troubles in your new home.

Andreas: Do we have an appointment?

Lakshmi: No (*laughing and waving her hand*), do we need an appointment for this; it is just a friendly gesture outside my work hours because I care about you and I have come all this way out of town to your house by autorickshaw to see if the landlord had supplied you the plants you wanted around your pool. (*Walks into the house and comments*) What a lovely house, nice and bright; you have arranged it all so tastefully.

Andreas (*still stern but shocked and angered as well at the unexpected entry*): Could you please leave now; it is Saturday afternoon and my wife and I want to spend some quiet time.

Lakshmi (*tears welling up*): OK, Andreas, I can see I am not welcome. Sorry.

Lakshmi then resigned from her job as she felt she couldn't work with Westerners. Andreas then stopped working with Lakshmi's company which had been so helpful earlier and a cultural distance built up.

* * *

How could this have been avoided? There are a few ways in which both parties could have sustained relationships.

Managing expectations: Telling the Westerner in more detail about the frustrations to expect about the house. This could have been reinforced even more.

When there is any project or collaborative effort required, it is good to lay out all expectations on both sides and not have anything unsaid. Then it is best to establish timelines which are realistic, given the slower process flow, potentially adding 100 per cent extra time if required. An honest answer is always better than a polite one as far as Westerners are concerned. For us too in India it is better to lay our cards on the table, making every effort to then stick to commitments. Communicating regularly, even if it means giving status quo or bad news of further delay, is required in a proactive format. A progress report tracker sheet should be maintained and exchanged weekly or even daily on efforts made for completion and follow up.

Knowing what Westerners would like: Privacy and permission. When Lakshmi couldn't reach them on the phone, she could have sent a handwritten note showing her care and offering to visit. What is acceptable in our culture may not be tolerated or may even go down negatively in another. For example, privacy and its invasion are two concepts which differ vastly in India and Western countries.

Reading body language: Once on the scene, when a question like 'Do we have an appointment' is uttered and there is no friendly invitation to enter the home, Lakshmi could have apologized and left at the gate.

What is unsaid is as important as what is said. Sensitizing ourselves cross-culturally will mean living in awareness and we will be far more mindful of the reactions at all levels. This allows fewer errors to be committed, unlike in the case of Lakshmi who dug herself deeper into the hole.

Adapting to local practices: Once Andreas saw Lakshmi was already there, he could have remembered this is the Indian way to overextend and drop by in person. He could have either welcomed her or if he really couldn't deal with her company just then, which is entirely understandable, he could have said 'thank you for coming' but explained that he was not going to be able to ask her in right then. He could have offered a more detailed explanation instead of cold monosyllabic answers. The adaptation has to be both ways and we have to walk towards the world to meet it halfway.

Insights for Outsiders:

Make the sugar coating thick.

In India, it is important to realize that the personal and professional are often mixed and a comment about a job could be taken as a personal affront. It is crucial to respect the person and allow him to save face even if the job isn't what you had expected. Affirm the person, then critique the action. The boss is seen as a patriarch; the client, as extended family; and the vendor, as a friend. Giving short blunt orders is perceived as outright rude and couching it in pleasantries is a must. Tolerance will be even lower if an outsider says things rather than an Indian boss. Relationship is valued above all else while doing business in India.

PART 2

Outsiders Inside

> 'As the traveller who has once been from home is wiser than he who has never left his own doorstep, so a knowledge of one other culture should sharpen our ability to scrutinize more steadily, to appreciate lovingly, our own.'
>
> —Margaret Meade, American anthropologist

This section is the fruit of journeys and an invitation to one for readers. If you like you can simply read it as a collection of tales from a real traveller but if you are able to remember some of it when you next step out on a journey yourself, then my book and writing would have served a double purpose.

There is a superb talent in Indians to be culturally adaptable human resources because we come with our own differences from Kashmir to Kanyakumari. This translates so beautifully in our being able to perform as cultural chameleons in places ranging from America to Japan. I will touch on a few life lessons learnt as we met people from those geographies right here in India.

1

OCCIDENT CALLING

What Works with Westerners

Cues to understanding the Western style of functioning: Westerners don't understand indirect communicators. If you can't do something you simply have to use the word 'no' in the sentence.

A participant at one of my training sessions wrote the following email to an American client:

Dear Karen,

Thank you for your mail. Will wait for your response and feedback.

Warm regards.

Pushpa C.

After reading her email, I shared these business writing tips with her:

- Use the word 'email' when you refer to it. Mail means regular post in the US.
- Use the subject 'I' and complete sentences; treating emails with the same respect as any other business document makes a good impression. 'I will wait for your response' is how line two in the mail should read.
- The signature could have just said 'Pushpa' or the full

name 'Puspha Chandra'. An initial appearing after a name is strange in most Western countries.

After receiving these tips, Pushpa asked, 'What else do I need to know when I work with Western people?' So I decided to share comments on 'Americans at work'. This is also the title of a book by cross-cultural guru Craig Storti, now a mentor of mine in Washington DC. He is American by birth and deeply sensitive about Easterners too. What he shares about country people could broadly apply to many Western countries too. How Westerners behave at work and how to deal with them comes through in these insightful tips. I have his permission to share them with you.

Here are two specific communication dos and don'ts that one must follow while working with the world.

SAY THE WORD 'NO'

Most Westerners don't understand indirect communicators: If you can't do something you simply *have to* use the word 'no' in the sentence. No other nicety will drive home the point. For example:

Bob: Are we still on schedule?

Nitin: Oh yes, we are working very hard on it.

Bob: Great, my teams are excitedly waiting to see the finished product.

If you think you didn't really commit because you indicated that the project was running late with the phrase 'we are working very hard', then you are wrong. The listener heard the 'Oh yes' you said but not the 'no' you did not say, and presumes it will be given on time. When you don't deliver, there will be fireworks!

Insight for Outsiders:

Reading between the Yes-es

'Yes' may not mean 'yes, it will be done'. Dig for deeper understanding, paraphrase and ask again to be sure what you heard was what was meant: 'Are you saying yes, you are listening, or yes, it will be ready by 4 p.m.?' Say 'I, as the foreigner, don't understand, and am making sure.' Blame it on yourself but curtail ambiguity by reconfirming. Tune your ear, so that you don't resort to filtered hearing. It could take the first few months but once you make this the practice, chances are you will do better. Encourage the speaker to share news that is not positive too by telling him/her in so many words.

AVOID UNDERSTATEMENTS

In India, we often talk of a 'small suggestion' or something being a 'little difficult'. Westerners will give this no value while you are trying to save face by understating the matter. If you mention how complicated the job is or how the last time another team had helped you in the hope that he gets the message and offers help this time too, it simply won't happen. If you need help ask for it directly and boldly, and simply use the word 'Please'. For example, 'John, I find this task tough. Can you please work on it with me?' John may say 'sure' or 'not right now' but will clearly know what you need.

DON'T SAY YOU UNDERSTAND IF YOU DON'T

Americans don't mind if you say you didn't understand when they say something. But they do mind when you say you understood and then find you actually didn't.

IF YOU HAVE A BETTER IDEA, SAY SO

John: Let's go ahead and use the alpha file for this project.

Ashok: John, I don't agree with using alpha. Beta is a better solution. We tested it in our lab.

Insight for Outsiders:

No Questions, Please!

The Indian education system teaches you to toe the line and not ask powerful questions. So the chances are that unless much encouragement is given, Indian team members will stay silent, or will ask among themselves to save face rather than own up they didn't understand.

Remember, Westerners will not understand any of the following techniques that you and I may employ if we want to disagree on a subject:

ASKING A LOT OF QUESTIONS

John: Let's use the alpha file.

Ashok: Oh, do you mean the alpha file which we used for the last project? Which we had in the Delhi and Bangalore teams? Will it work out fast enough?

CHANGING THE SUBJECT

John: Let's use the alpha file.

Ashok: I sent the update on the other project also to your team last evening.

ANSWERING A QUESTION WITH ANOTHER QUESTION

John: You will use the alpha file for this project, right?

Ashok: Why are we doing this programme in html?

SAYING NOTHING

Silence will be taken as agreement, not doubt as you may have intended.

So if you say things bluntly it will actually work because they will only think it is direct, and through their cultural lens it is not rude or blunt as it may seem to us in India. What is viewed rude is to say nothing when we have the chance, and then not to be able to deliver.

I know when Westerners are direct, we Indians sometimes think they are rude and this is one area where they need to soften. The middle ground needs to be reached and we simply have to be aware that we look at the world from two different cultural viewpoints. Adapting both our styles to meet midway makes for effective communication.

What Else Works with Westerners

More tips for understanding the Western way

The second part of 'meeting halfway' in communication is here as a few more tips for working successfully with Westerners. I find that I have so much to share on working with Westerners!

BE PROACTIVE ABOUT PROBLEM-SOLVING

Westerners talk only in terms of 'challenges', not failures or problems. So, if as the Indian on the team, you think through a situation and come up with suggestions to solve it showing true commitment to resolve issues, you will succeed at working in a team with Western colleagues or customers. Your proactive, 'can do' attitude will gel well.

SOUND POSITIVE

So the first step is to have enthusiasm and the right attitude to solve issues. But it is not enough if this enthusiasm is only in your mind. You need to articulate it loud and clear, which is the crucial Step Two. Stating something negative may make them feel you are being pessimistic. Instead, always say 'This is how we can fix this.' Never say 'This is not going to work.'

If you say 'John, we have already used this alpha programme in Delhi but it was too slow and complicated,' he doesn't hear your positive note. Instead say 'John, because I know from the last project that the alpha programme is slow, I am going to (shows you are going to take positive action) brainstorm with my team to see if beta or delta would be more suitable. Give me (note the usage of action-oriented words!) two days to get back to you with a positive solution.'

DON'T WORRY TOO MUCH ABOUT MISTAKES

When things go wrong, just get up and start again. Don't complain or make excuses. When a child falls down in India, the mother often says, 'Bad floor, why did you trip my baby?' She may even go on to smack the floor a couple of times, to stop her baby's crying. On the other hand, a British or American mother's comment is likely to be: 'I am so sorry baby; you must watch where you are going next time!'

This child-rearing practice builds a tendency to transfer blame and is carried through into adulthood too. In our work life, we look around to see who is responsible for a delay or a goof-up. On the other hand, the Westerner learns accountability and simply apologizes, moving on as there is no great stigma attached to failing.

When this Westerner and Indian meet on the same team in adult life and need to work together, the Indian's tendency to complain and make excuses when he makes a mistake will simply not be acceptable to the Westerner. What he may accept though is: 'I am sorry, John, that we could not meet today's deadline; it is my mistake as I misjudged the effort. I will bring in extra hands and give you a customer-ready product by Tuesday

4 p.m.'. It is hard for us Indians to articulate this way and it requires practice. But if you do (and deliver at 4 p.m. you must), then success is yours and the mistake is forgotten!

The other day I came across a beautiful Sanskrit word in the Bhagavad Gita: 'Eeksha'. Meaning 'right judgment', it is a great value to live by. In cross-cultural relations, it enables us to find the right balance. A person with Eeksha assesses the pros and cons of the situation and wisely follows the middle path. Sometimes he adapts to the Western way, sometimes he doesn't, knowing fully what to expect. And then, there are times, when he gets the Westerner to adapt to his ways!

2

WESTERN VIEW

Customer Service Lessons from Barack Obama

A perfectly worded thank-you note delivered in the nick of time

The American political landscape was historically transformed following Barack Obama's election as the US President. So what is the first lesson to learn from Barack Obama? Customer service and follow-up!

'Your call is important to us . . . Please don't hang up . . . Our customer executive will be with you in a few minutes . . .' Now, be honest. What is your reaction to a taped voice assuring you some ten times over that your call is important? Aren't you tempted to hang up? The next time you call and get the same message, you'll hang up without waiting for the tape to reach round two.

Your irritation is entirely warranted; you're within your rights in thinking that you have better things to do with your time than listen to a recorded voice spouting meaningless sentiment. You'd be justified in looking elsewhere for what you need. The fallout for the original service provider is, of course, loss of business.

Shortage of staff was most probably the reason you got the taped message in response to your call, yet keeping the two 'Ps' in mind is very important to all our business strategies. The first 'P' is 'Professionalism' and the second 'P' is 'Personal touch'. As a new manager, you will need to make sure that your organization has the right number of people with the right attitude to attend to customers' requirements promptly and efficiently.

SUPERB TIMING

In this context, I'd like to quote an email that Barack Obama sent each of his campaigners after his victory was announced. Obviously, it had been prepared in advance and Obama had made arrangements using technology to personalize each mail and send it out. But the beauty is the addressees got it just minutes before he made his acceptance speech. It was a small, superbly timed and important part of the elaborate strategy that put the first African-American in the White House and so made history.

Here it is:

> Kamini—
>
> I'm about to head to Grant Park to talk to everyone gathered there, but I wanted to write to you first. We just made history. And I don't want you to forget how we did it. You made history every single day during this campaign—every day you knocked on doors, made a donation or talked to your family, friends and neighbours about why you believe it's time for change. I want to thank all of you who gave your time, talent and passion to this campaign. We have a lot of work to do to get our country back on track and I'll be in touch soon about what comes next. But I want to be very clear about one thing . . . All of this happened because of you.
>
> Thank you,
>
> Barack

Note the planning which went into this exercise. Note the wording, calculated to make each one feel special and therefore ready to give continued support: a calculated public relations measure from a master tactician. I wholeheartedly appreciate the thought that went into it and the wonderful results this relatively easy step is sure to have generated.

The same principles can be used and extended to draw up your winning strategy for customer service too—give personalized service wherever possible; get to know your customers by name; you could even remember their families' details or their hobbies. Put in a little extra service when possible so they'll feel they're getting into a relationship that is above mere business. This way you're ensuring customer loyalty. Our customer relations manager has a smile that reaches up to her eyes and says *terve* and *kiitos* ('welcome' and 'thank you') to all our telecom clients from Finland and each time, she gets a loyal customer on her side.

Also, one last point about Obama's email: It was, in a sense, a follow-up effort. Follow-up is an essential part of customer service. When you have concluded a deal or provided the service the customer sought, the story shouldn't end there. You need to find out if the customer is happy, anticipating and offering solutions to further challenges. By doing this, you are keeping lines of communication open for repeat business.

For instance, we once helped a single, Finnish woman who had moved to an Indian city settle into her new home. When our manager called her a week later, she found her down with relocation blues. Our Finnish client had been to a beach with a large number of poor people on it and had been overwhelmed by India. A visit to our office, a cuppa and a chat fixed her morale and sealed our friendship forever. We always have time for our customers, even when they don't ask for it.

Successful customer service is thus a well thought-out series of measures, sincere in its intent yet a great strategy aimed at ensuring a satisfied clientele which keeps coming back for more.

Striking the Right Chord

Avoiding conversational gaffes, especially with Westerners, is easier with these tips.

Take interest in their interest but 'don't ask personal questions'. This seems to be a contradiction. But what exactly are 'personal questions'? How 'personal' is personal?

Sometimes, we Indians think nothing of asking others personal questions or indeed of providing personal information about ourselves, our families, our employers or employees to casual acquaintances and perhaps even to perfect strangers, such as a fellow traveller on a train.

Insight for Outsiders:

What to ask and what not to ask . . .

Asking about age, salary, price of a piece of clothing or artefact is considered 'taking interest' and modern Indians too squirm under these direct questions. But be aware that there are instances where this sort of questioning is not given a second thought. 'How many children do you have? Why only two? Is something wrong?' These may well be questions from those in their sixties in India. The young Indian has become sophisticated and urbanized and may not ask as much. However, the rural migratory Indian, even though young, may end up asking such things. All you have to do is to smile and say half-jokingly, 'It is a secret,' and get out of the dicey situation.

Generally speaking, the expatriate in India finds this aspect of conversation with Indians difficult to digest. When small talk turns to subjects like age, assets and health, for instance, they see it as an invasion of privacy and will either avoid further conversation or snub the questioner in no uncertain terms. This in turn will lead to the Indian taking offence as he loses face, and much damage is done on both sides.

To understand the Western reticence, it would perhaps help us Indians to simply go back to our own roots which we have not paid attention to in the flurry of modernity and growth. Hindu scriptures, over 3000 years ago, talked about seven *parama gopya* or supreme secrets that are not supposed to be discussed. Curiously these secrets match with the taboos of conversational topics considered 'bad form' with Westerners.

In the workplace, we tend to easily cross the line between the personal and professional; at such times, let's stay away from these seven topics which are sensitive:

Age: It is considered rude to ask how old a person is, in casual conversation. Also, it isn't good manners to ask about the age difference between a husband and wife; often, in the West, women are older than their husbands (less common in India) and the couple may not want to say so.

Wealth: In the course of small talk, never ask an expatriate how much he or she earns or what his or her assets are. It will be considered unforgivably rude.

Family situation: Don't ask for information on the marital status or number of offspring. In India, such questions are taken as an expression of friendliness and interest but in the West they're viewed differently. Family ties also often vary from our perception of them; for instance, chances of children from different marriages are more common in other cultures than in India.

I remember being horrified when a Frenchman to whom I casually mentioned that my son worked with 'his' father immediately assumed that I was referring to my ex-husband! I had not taken into account the fact that divorce is taken far more for granted as a possibility in the West than in India. To make the situation clear, I ought to have said 'My son works with my husband.' Such erroneous assumptions can work both ways and cause avoidable embarrassment.

Faith: A Westerner will not take kindly to questions regarding his religion. To understand this sentiment, think how we would feel if they asked us which caste we belonged to. We would think it an impertinent question and they hold the same view on questions about their religious beliefs.

Sex and reproduction: These topics are off-limits, and asking a husband or wife personal details about his or her spouse is in complete bad taste.

Similarly, bawdy humour is alien to the Indian culture and if we have adopted Western swear words with sexual overtones in the belief that they are needed to express ourselves clearly to the Westerner, remember such vocabulary is both unnecessary and often not appreciated by anyone. The rule of thumb is to speak to others as you would have them speak to you.

Health: Specific questions or comments about health are also considered unwarranted by Westerners. If you do see evidence of a medical problem—say a white patch on the person's skin—desist from commenting or offering free advice. It would be best to ignore it.

Charity: Don't ask how much someone has donated to any charity or cause. Such questions will be seen as unnecessarily pandering to the ego. As the saying goes, 'The left hand should not know what the right hand has given.'

If we follow these don'ts, we can easily stay away from conversational topics that could become pitfalls for us. The taboos hold good not only for conversations with business associates and colleagues, even if we think we have come to know them very well, but also with friends and even close family members.

'So then what do we talk about,' you might ask. The rules of etiquette prescribe many safe topics for small talk in the Western world. The weather is the proverbial neutral conversational gambit. Sports and hobbies are other topics that are sure to strike a chord with most people and draw them out. Current affairs, provided they're not too controversial; holidays and festivals; your respective hometowns; and general talk about each other's occupation usually go down well too.

If we follow these general rules of conversation, we're sure to fare well in interpersonal relations.

Insight for Outsiders:

The art of (Indian) small talk

In India it is taboo to talk about dating or sex with young people even in jest, with parents around; it is better not to ask about poverty, comment on political parties or delve deep into caste. It is good conversation to ask about travel experiences of Indians, where their children go or went to college and to discuss festivals or films. Don't ask for recipes of the hostess, for example, as her cook may have made the dinner; do comment on artefacts or lovely home layouts. And don't be surprised if you are given a tour of the rest of the house. When Indians come to your place, do show them around if you feel comfortable. Make enough dishes to fill the table and offer food and drink repeatedly—refilling glasses and plates. Expect similar gushy hospitality too.

Winning over a Foreign Client

Basic courtesies and an idea of foreign traditions will be of help.

Being well behaved and doing things as expected may not get you noticed or earn you brownie points but not doing things as expected will certainly get you attention for the wrong reasons. So there's positive attention and negative attention. Holding the fork in the right hand, wearing a brown suit for a formal dinner—which is not done in the West—or not saying 'please' or 'thank you' are all going to make a new Indian manager stick out in a foreign scenario.

We need to be able to adapt in order to interact with different cultures, so that we don't do something which is so glaringly different or do them so many times that only the differences stand out. Instead, we should do what is expected—in this sense we exceed all expectations by doing it well.

'Fine, fine, I will do it,' you'll say. 'What do you want me to do?' Well, the first step to adaptation is knowledge. Let's look at a few ways to do the right things. Below's a list I've put together from years of experience running cultural awareness programmes at Global Adjustments.

FOR AMERICA, SITUATIONAL HUMOUR WORKS

I remember the time I was at the Harvard COOP, a bookstore established in 1882 which continues to charge its members the original fee of one dollar. The place is filled with a spirit that encourages learning and sharing. I was there to participate in its 'Meet the Author' series held on weekday nights, where I did a quick India update on my book *Doing Business in India for Dummies.* I started out with a mention of the unchanged membership fee of one dollar at the COOP and how it has not affected inflation and been respectful of the economy. It hooked my audience, a motley lot of Americans of various ethnic origins.

FOR GERMANY, TIMELINESS AND EFFICIENCY WORK

In the corridors of Frankfurt airport, I wheeled my bag and watched the signs on the ceiling to see which way my gate is. I bumped into the security officer, who warned me, 'Lady, always watch where you are going.' He was right of course. How many times have I shared with students in my class the importance of living in awareness when we are overseas—of where we are headed; of people who may be walking by us; of whether we are blocking exits as we look up signs, and the like. Yet here I was, guilty as charged! (Hey, I never said I was perfect.)

So where's the hook for Germany? While working with our German clients on a training programme in Bangalore, we sent them, as a daily update, a tracker sheet on the progress made under various heads of the project. Besides, we also sent them a weekly overview. On a day when we did not have much to report, we simply sent them a one-line email saying, 'The project is on track; we will include today's actions in tomorrow's report.' We followed up on this assurance. They were impressed with our promptness and meticulous reporting. Now, we have been chosen as their suppliers for other cities in India.

FOR JAPAN, DEFERENTIAL BEHAVIOUR AND OBSERVING THE NICETIES WORK

Fujitsu, a client, is sending an official who will be based in India. When I greet the HR exploratory team with the right bow and a perfect card exchange; sit only after they are seated; compliment the leader on his good English; and tell him sincerely how much I like the Japanese language and culture, adding the little phrases I know, I have the team hooked to my primary agenda.

FOR FRANCE, SMALL TALK AROUND THE TABLE WORKS

When this Indian businessman who is known to us consulted us on a potential merger and acquisition possibility for his company, we explained to him the three-hour business lunch concept. He and his company director invited the French company to a meal and, course after course, talked about the art, regions and wines of France, simply showing an interest in their country. It cemented the relationship. When the French company's interest in the Indian company was sustained, they did the right thing by escorting the Indian businessman from London to Paris in a Eurostar: buying him the ticket, picking him up in a cab and accompanying him to the Parisian office. These are small but meaningful gestures that cement relations the Indian way. Both sides made the right effort and are now happily united.

Insight for Outsiders:

Talking of family . . .

For India, specifically, relationships and conversations work. Two Americans had taken two Indian engineers out for a buffet luncheon. It was clear our Indian friends were not comfortable with either the fork-and-knife routine or the small talk over the meal. But the Americans cleverly steered the conversation and asked questions like, 'So what does your sister do? And what about your "co-brother" (the wife's sister's husband)?'

They had picked up the terminology we use to denote different relationships. This instantly relaxed the Indians who were soon in the mood to rattle on about their family members, their degrees and awards. Camaraderie was established. After all, it takes two to make a deal. Theirs was a happy relationship too.

In a nutshell, when you know you have to strike up a business relationship with people from a different culture, do your homework about what works and what does not (that's equally important) in that culture. Plan ahead, strategize, figure out exactly how you will behave, what tone you will take and what you will say at meetings. Learn, practise and prepare your behaviour. Then the business automatically happens.

This is worth repeating—business skills and behavioural skills are simply two sides of the same coin which denotes success.

3

EASTWARD HO!

Eastern Elements

Some pointers about what makes the Far East tick—take a cue, India!

SINGAPORE

I was very keen to get international business for my company from American relocation giants. To my surprise, I found that the decision makers who use vendors out of India were located in Singapore. It is the hub for Asia-Pacific business interactions to many a Fortune 500 company. So I brushed up on my best Singapore etiquette and went out to conquer the world.

When I had some time, I decided to go and look around the campuses and observe the lifestyle and value systems of the young Singaporeans, who are going to be tomorrow's business force. Here are three basic things that struck me in the campuses:

Hard-working and people-oriented

- Relationships are important for Singaporeans and hence they make it a point to interact with people. So, as a student, you would be able to make friends for a lifetime.
- Singaporeans are more westernized in their work approach than Indians. I have come across some Singaporeans of Chinese origin who are efficient, hard-working and process-oriented.

Some dos and don'ts

- Singapore is a crowded country, yet they like to maintain a certain physical distance while talking in a business or campus environment. It creates a sense of comfort for them.
- Maintain handshaking distance between you and the speaker.
- In spite of crowds, discipline is visible everywhere you go. The entire city is spotless. Chewing gum and littering are punishable offences in Singapore. You will be fined heavily if you are found littering or if you do not flush after using the toilet.
- Time consciousness and punctuality are part of the 'to do' attitude. In class, do not interrupt, be brief in your explanations, and be prepared.

'Can do' attitude

- Education is a significant aspect in an individual's life and within society. This accounts for higher standards of education in Singapore.
- They expect efficiency in work. They are driven by the need to perform and excel.

Singapore's neighbours—Malaysia, Hong Kong and Korea—share many of its traditions and customs. But there are some things that are emphasized more in one or another of these Eastern powerhouses of business. A few insider tips could go a long way.

KOREA

In Korea, which holds a big place in world economy and has a strong share of the expatriate business pie in India, relationships are very important. So stress on past and present ties if you want to make a good impression. Another way of looking at it is the value Koreans place on the human factor—it beats the bottom line any time. Protocol and hierarchy are super important too. Just like in India, the Koreans place premium value on respect for those who are older and senior.

The concept of face is very highly valued here, so keep that in mind when you're dealing with the Koreans.

Two quick tips

- Don't push yourself and your achievements forward. Learn to take a back seat and defer to others.
- Give the people you are interacting with your full attention. The Koreans don't take kindly to those who are distracted or keep losing focus.

HONG KONG

Hong Kong, which was for long a British colony and therefore capitalist, has been returned to China and now functions as a sort of via media between socialism and capitalism. It has its business flavour.

- The Chinese influence can be seen in the importance given to feng shui and the significance of colours. Red is a preferred shade, so a red tie for your first business meeting would go down very well.
- Handshakes are important, and if you make a slight bow while you're doing it it will strike the right note of respect.
- Toasts are mandatory, so don't refuse a drink even if you're a teetotaller. Just accept it for the purpose of toasting.
- Expect some periods of silence at your business meets. Don't expect quick decisions.
- Beware if you hear your Hong Kong associates sucking air in audibly through their mouth or teeth—sounding something like as if they've burnt their tongues on hot

tea—it's a signal that they're upset. So quickly rethink whatever you were saying.

MALAYSIA

As for Malaysia, it is a mix of three cultures—Chinese, Indian and Malay. Obviously, the cultures of all three intermingle here, and you might have to do some quick chopping and changing depending on the origins of your business associates. But there are some common rules you would do well to keep in mind:

- Be formal till you get a feel of how your associates want the business to go.
- If there are women in the team you are dealing with, wait till they extend their hand before offering to shake hands. If you are a woman in Malaysia, remember that many Malaysian men would prefer to bow to a woman with a hand on their hearts rather than shake hands with her. It would be safest to follow your associates' lead in this.
- When you go for a meeting let the senior-most in your team lead the way in, so he or she can interact immediately with the seniors on the opposite side. It is a way of showing respect, and will be well received. Pointing with the forefinger is never to be done; Malays point with the thumb while the rest of the fingers are held in a fist.
- Beware if you hear your Malaysian associates laugh at places you feel are inappropriate. They are most probably trying to cover up feelings of apprehension. Try to figure out what might have caused this feeling, and see how you can allay their fears.

This story of St Francis of Assisi strikes a nice chord of the holistic approach. Once St Francis was walking down a street and saw labourers working: 'What are you doing my good man?'

he asked each in turn. 'Putting up bricks and spreading cement on them,' said the first; 'Building a wall,' said the second; 'Creating the most beautiful cathedral in Florence,' said the third. So too when we have interpersonal interactions with other cultures we can think 'I am just doing my job as a software engineer' or 'I am representing my country' or 'I am an Indian cultural ambassador representing my company and country'.

So I watch what I say, when I say and how I say it to make a good impression for all those I stand for.

Gelling with the Japanese

The Japanese aren't so different from us Indians in many things, though they do have their own unique customs and traditions. Knowledge of traditions is important for building a good business rapport.

One of my very first Japanese clients of over a decade ago came back to visit India and set me thinking on what I had learnt to do right which cemented our relationship. Other than providing high quality at the right price and meeting deadlines, there are ten things which, if done right, help in gelling with the Japanese.

1. *Making sounds of empathy* is what they do often—ahhh, soooooo—you don't have to do it unless you can make it a natural practice but respect their style of responses, which are slower and thoughtful and have many pauses with empathetic sounds.
2. *Slowing down your speech*: Of all the races we Indians are often accused of speaking too fast—especially when uttering words we are very familiar with we tend to let them roll off our tongues so fast. I remember telling one of my Japanese clients that *satyameva jayate* was our Indian national slogan and it meant 'Truth alone

triumphs'. He was very interested but had to ask me to repeat it at least eight times before getting it. Finally I wrote it down and he deliberately and seriously repeated each syllable 'sat-ya-me-va ja-ya-te–truth-alone-triumphs'. I could have made it easier by slowing down myself in the first place.

3. *Thanking them* for the last time when you next meet is as important as saying thank you when an act is done. I had taken my Japanese client out for dinner to the Taj hotel and when we met again almost a month later, the first thing he said was 'Thank you for our dinner last time at the Taj—the nan bread was very good.' It not only made me feel happy but I also realized that this was a Japanese nicety as an icebreaker. If you get your speaker happy with a compliment and gratitude for an act from the past, it gets him or her ready to listen to you and be attentive to your needs this time around too. So do find something to thank them to make sure this meeting goes well.
4. *Bowing Japanese style*: The bow for the man is: hands by the side, straight and pointing to the heels; eyes looking to the ground. For the woman the hands are held in front of the thighs clasped lightly as she bows; eyes, towards the ground. Keeping your eyes upwards trying to maintain eye contact is actually considered very rude. So practise this several times till you become comfortable; it is worth the effort.
5. Offer *similarities between Japan and India* as a conversation starter. Many of our clients in Marubeni Corporation in the early days became my friends through conversations we had on how we believed in eldercare and respect for age in our two countries. We also discussed how well we followed traditional ceremonies in both cultures such as the tea ceremony in theirs or a pooja in ours. Tea

drinking was relationship- and respect-building for both sides. Just this sort of knowledge helps.

6. *Exchange of business cards* is super important of course. The Japanese may think of his business card as his own face or identity, so do not shove it into your back pocket and sit on it; it is as insulting as someone sitting on your face! Take a few minutes to read contents, utter the name slowly with *san* at the end, place it in front of you to refer to it from time to time. Try it out with your own Indian colleagues; it feels good to have paid and received attention actually. Hand and receive cards with both hands holding the two corners, name pointing towards receiver: this is not to hide the name with a clumsy finger-hold and to enable the receiver to see the name right away. Print your cards in Japanese too if you are doing long-term business with Japan. It helps build relationships.
7. *Learning a few phrases* in any language is helpful but is particularly easy and has a huge impact with Japan so I highly recommend it. Here is a short list; the Internet can show you pronunciations but chances are you will get it right anyway as words are mostly pronounced the way they are written: *oishii desu ne*—it (any food or drink they offer) is so tasty; *eigo wa ojozu desu ne*—how good your English is! *Itadakimasu*—an expression to use before you start your meal while dining with the Japanese; *gochisosama deshita*—the meal was delicious (used after a meal); *konnichi wa*—good day; *komban wa*—good evening; *domo arigato gozaimasu*—thank you very much.
8. *Use the suffix san for all Japanese last names* but never for your own. So I found that Fukase san could be used for Wataru Fukase the man or Yukiko Fukase the woman when we refer to them by last name. But you could also refer to people by their first names—I could ask, for

example, 'Watarusan, how is Yukikosan doing?' or vice versa. You never give too much importance to yourself so you would never say 'I am Ranjinisan' as I found out the hard way with much giggling among my Japanese women friends when I first uttered it! ('ko' is the ending for Japanese women's names like 'ini' often is for Indian women's first names.)

9. *Make relevant small talk*: Buddhist places in India, Indian films and festivals like holi and diwali are topics Japanese enjoy; keep short sentences handy to describe each of these and it will be a great conversation filler. Ask them about *sakura*—their cherry blossom flower—and about Mount Fuji (*Fujisan*) which they venerate as we do the Himalayas. Say how you would love to see *Fujisan* one day . . . it is breathtakingly beautiful. Similarities you can use as icebreakers include *hinamatsuri*, a doll festival like we have *kolu* in south India, and the use of rice as staple food. They even use rice balls for their death ceremonies like we do in India.
10. *Wait to be seated at restaurants* and meetings and ask where before you sit. Bow many times and thank profusely. It stays well with the Japanese.

By the time I got back from Japan I had really let the culture soak into my skin because I found myself bowing even on the telephone! It was funny in retrospect but, remember, never make fun of another culture: laugh with them, never at them. I have allowed laughing at only one person: *myself*. It works in the Global Indian cultural context.

PART 3

Let's Get Down to Business

'Culture is the widening of the mind and of the spirit'
—Jawaharlal Nehru

Like the layers of an onion which hold the same fragrance of the core, behavioural skills and business skills offer the essence of a successful Global Indian. Layer one is understanding our own culture, acknowledging what makes us tick and why we do things the way we do. This helps us in two ways: explain ourselves to others and, second, knowing where we are can get us to where we want to be.

The second layer is understanding the other side of our world, not a better side or a lower side, not the right side or the wrong side but just a different side so that we can adapt to working successfully with them.

The third layer now is in the fine art of communication. A Global Indian works at getting it right—in speaking, writing, making presentations, meeting people, 'mobiling' or 'mousing'! Communication includes the spoken, written and the unspoken word. Body language, facial expressions—all count. Let's explore a few of the best practices through stories we have experienced.

1

COMMUNICATION MATTERS

Getting It Right

Communication is a two-way process that can deliver immense benefit.

It's all about communication. With technology advancing in leaps and bounds, communication, of both the wired and the wireless sort is virtually a button away. Accessibility has increased beyond anybody's imagination and you can almost instantly get anyone's ear, from the President of your country to the booking clerk at the nearest railway station.

Ideally, communication is a two-way street. As business people, we need to put ourselves across to our clientele. How else will they know what we have to offer? Equally, our clientele needs to reach us; how else will we know what they have to say? I'm going to pull a few tips from an occupant of the White House.

In the West people appreciate the importance of two-way communication, which could serve as a model for India to do more than we do at present. Consider this email sent from the former US President Bill Clinton's address to those who had backed Hillary Clinton's candidature as the Democratic Party's presidential nominee:

Dear Kamini,

I am sure you have heard the exciting news: Hillary Clinton is nominated to be our next Secretary of State! This is great news for our country. She understands the challenges we face and her experience and judgement will help President Obama restore America's reputation in the world and make our nation more secure. Take a moment to celebrate this wonderful news by sending Hillary a message of congratulations. This nomination would not have been possible without the hard work of everyone like you who has supported Hillary throughout the years. I know I speak for her when I say thank you for everything you have done for her.

Sincerely,

Bill Clinton

A link in this mail took you to a site with a button which said 'Congratulate Hillary'. By clicking the button, you could do just that and type out your message. Wouldn't you be excited to receive such a personalized email if you were Kamini, and wouldn't you have used the link straightaway? Hillary Clinton's core team is ensuring that communication channels between Hillary and her supporters are kept open because the team understands the value of a two-way flow.

L-A-C-E

Too often in our busy schedules, we limit our communications to a single direction. But this way, we're cutting off an important resource. For best results on both sides—company and client—we have followed from experts in our Global Indian programme the acronym LACE: listen, acknowledge, clarify, explain.

Do not only allow but also help the client/customer talk to you. Listen to the concerns/views that he or she expresses, acknowledge the feedback, clarify the situation if you have to and explain your position. This interaction will work to help the two sides understand each other better, and ensure better results and mutual satisfaction in the future. No customer/client should be considered too small or unimportant to be a part of this exercise. Bill Clinton's email was sent out to each and every person who played a part in Hillary's campaign, no matter how minor.

I know you will wonder: Won't important messages get lost in the flood? Ease of accessibility is a good thing from the point of view of those who want to be heard. But those who are doing the hearing often wonder if it's not more of a bane than a boon. But even this can be tackled if thought is put into writing the email, to leave an impression and to get the desired responses. Since email is now more or less the preferred form of both inter- and intra-office communication, let's take a simple example. This is an email from my expatriate employee requesting leave of absence for a few days:

> I am writing to ask your permission to take a few days leave over Christmas and New Year, (*note that she states the purpose of the email in the very first sentence, respecting the importance of time for a busy person to get the gist of the email as soon as it is opened)* as I hope to discover some areas of Rajasthan during this time (*she gives the reason clearly*).
>
> More specifically, the period in question is from Thursday, 25 December to Sunday, 4 January, which amounts to five working days' leave (*she gives the dates, and recaps it with exact numbers so that there is clarity in the message*).
>
> All my work that needs to be completed before January, I can coordinate together with my manager (*she takes responsibility and addresses the issue that is bound to be on the boss's mind, thus making the decision to say 'yes' easy*). I hope that this will be possible (*the tone is polite and respectful without being overly humble*).
>
> Thank you

Official communication that meets the parameters, like this

exemplary email leave application does, is sure to hit the spot. I, for one, granted the leave and even gave the trip as part of a bonus gift I had planned for this hard-working and focused employee.

Communication is a powerful asset and, like any other resource, if harnessed correctly, can power huge progress. If you are precise, coherent, polite and proactive on the one hand and receptive on the other, this tool can only be a two-way boon.

Writing Essentials

With a little care you can use the email to convey a very good impression about yourself to your business associates.

An email we received at Global Adjustments went like this: 'It was pleasure to meet with you and team at your office and we herewith confirm the meeting on xx Jan xx. a.m. at our office to discuss the below said agenda mentioned in your mail and move forward. Mr XYZ, Head xx Solutions—South and Mr ABC, Head of our marketing team shall represent our company.'

'Below said agenda mentioned?' 'Herewith confirm?' I felt lost and my mind was in a tizzy about what had been said! Can't we simplify the language in the email and use that wonderful invention called the full stop or period? How about this: 'It was a pleasure to meet at your office. We are glad to confirm the next meeting at our office on xx. We look forward to discussing the agenda you proposed in your email.'

A professor of Cambridge University once remarked, 'The world's English will soon have Indian ways of speaking and writing and the use of American English will be overtaken by the "Inglish" style.' One example is the use of the present continuous tense that we in India are used to such as 'I am holding a degree in Communication' where the West says 'I hold a degree in Communication.' No pressing need to change that. The world is going to change to be on the same page as we are as we edge up to become leaders in business with the maximum number of English speakers, who are critical to the success of humanity as a whole.

Semantics doesn't really matter. Partha, a senior corporate leader who has travelled close to a hundred times to the UK, shared this experience with me. He requested 'light tea' from a British flight attendant who gently corrected him, asking if what he wanted was 'weak tea'. There is no longer a need to get it so right!

However, the three simple steps below work both for Indians and foreigners, and are needed to help us communicate rather than confuse.

BE BRIEF YET POLITE

Use fewer words when you write and speak, and chances are the message gets delivered quickly and effectively. Many times, two words meaning the same such as 'attached herewith' or 'herein below' can easily be trimmed down.

The other day, I heard a Westerner ask his young travel agent, 'Are you terribly busy or would you mind if we took the time now to have a look at the itinerary to Paris please?' Raghu, the agent, was lost in the trail of twenty-four words.

'Try again, John,' I said.

'Raghu, shall we look at that Paris itinerary please,' said John and Raghu shot out a beaming smile and a 'Sure Sir'.

Indians can be verbose too, rather than just saying 'It will take two days', we may hear a tailor saying 'It should be possible and I will work with this cloth first to complete it very soon for you.'

RESPECTFUL, NOT SUBSERVIENT, STYLE

There is no need to 'request your kind self'. Let us instead 'request 'you' or 'Mr P' or 'Sir' instead, using their name or title, which is more personal anyway. The days of 'humbly plead' are definitely gone and just saying 'please' works with a wonderful combination of clockwork efficiency and civility.

'We would introduce ourselves as leading suppliers' is not as effective as 'We are leading suppliers.' Claim assertively who you are and the world gives you its attention.

Westerners, au contraire, include words showing reverence for age, wisdom or stature, or simply show reverence for all other fellow human beings. One of the best mentors I learnt from is Sue Fox, the author of *Business Etiquette for Dummies.* She always signs off her email or autographs her books with 'respectfully'. Just one word but a world of meaning, and as a last word it makes a lasting impression.

USE PROPER GRAMMAR

Missing out articles like 'a' and 'the' in India, as seen in the sample email I started this story with, clearly does not create a good impression of you. These are easy to fix with practice and attention to detail.

Go back to the basics and learn. Apply it to all emails to make it a habit, even internal ones, even when you are in a short communication mode. Use spell check and reread before you hit SEND. Writing properly shows you are a thorough professional. I personally spend time training people in my company in this area and it has paid rich dividends. Here is a recent interaction between me and one of my most promising managers.

He wrote me a one-line email: 'We have a network problem, I am telling this because webmail seems to work well from outside the office, where the connectivity is good.' 'Dear ABC,' I wrote, 'we tell someone, something. We say something to someone. "Tell" is used only when there is "someone" following immediately after. That is the rule to remember. (Don't worry, I had to keep memorizing this in my early years—tell someone, say something; tell someone, say something; tell someone, say something . . .) So in the above sentence "I am telling *you* this because" would have been correct. "I am saying this because" would also have been correct.'

> **Insight for Outsiders:**
>
> *Don't KISS; we may misunderstand!*
>
> Westerners might use acronyms, turns of phrase or sports analogies which the reader may not necessarily know. Reducing such usages shows that the Westerner's intention is to have the Indian person understand. KISS—keep it simple and straightforward—might be one such.

Do stop a moment, reread and put yourself in the shoes of the person you are communicating with. Check for his ease of understanding.

Presenting the Art of Presentations

Present powerfully and leave them wanting more.

In these days of instant technology solutions, audiovisual presentations have become an essential communication aid. Be it board meetings or interviews, a guest lecture or a private function, making a presentation is mandatory.

The fact that it has become so common makes it all the more important that you master the art, for an art it is. Here are a few tips on making an effective presentation.

Don't become a victim of stage fright

Most of us have inhibitions about facing a crowd, and if major decisions hinge on our performance we are likely to feel queasy! To this large majority I say: there's nothing that you can't do with practice; I know because I worked hard myself. Develop your self-worth. Be at ease with yourself. It brings about self-confidence. Self-confidence shows as the audience picks up your body language. Work at it. Practise till you are comfortable with yourself in front of a mirror.

Once you reach a stage where you know that your voice is well modulated (tape your own voice and play it back to yourself), your posture, confident, and your dress-sense, faultless, stop worrying about these aspects. You will know it is time because people will tell you repeatedly about your voice and dress once you get it right. How do you overcome self-consciousness? I do it by immersing myself in what I am saying; I make eye contact with several in the audience, dwelling just a few seconds more to look into their eyes as I make my point. As for stage fright, take a deep breath, inhale and expand your stomach, exhale and push it in. (Tried that now? Yes, I know, this sequence seems in reverse to what we do; I fumbled for the first few times too. Yoga teaches us this correct form of deep stomach breathing.) Repeat as needed. It helps.

ATTENTION PLEASE!

Next, let's look at the presentation. Irrespective of the subject matter, there are some common guidelines that need to be followed to grab and keep audience attention.

The opening is important. Decide how you want your audience to connect with you. Many public speakers start with a joke—it relaxes the audience and makes them amenable to paying attention to the serious points you will be raising further along. But remember jokes about others run the risk of being counterproductive. Jokes about yourself work best. For instance, when I address a group of young professionals on cross-cultural communication, I often say, 'I know you think, what is this *mammi* (carrying the nuance of a staid lady) from Mylapore (an area in Chennai noted for being a hub of tradition) going to tell me about cross-culture?' That usually draws smiles all around. Then I quickly establish expert position, saying, 'Let me share with you how to build an xx-crore revenue company paying attention to relationship building, and to win a State Entrepreneur award'. So the audience takes you seriously.

PICTURE PERFECT

Journalism students are repeatedly told that a picture is worth a thousand words. A winning combination is to use pictures as well as the written and spoken word in an interactive way with questions to the audience instead of 'telling' them everything. But do use the power of being on stage wisely.

The other day I attended an inauguration where several important people were present in the audience. The speaker made a PowerPoint presentation and could have left a lasting impression on them. But his numerous slides were all packed with dry information. The font was tiny, the lines ran on and on, and people's eyes grew tired. They must have felt like echoing the words of the popular song 'Hotel California': *You can check out anytime but you can never leave.*

So break up your information into chunks that are easy on the eye and the mind.

Q&A

Know your audience beforehand. Research them on the Internet; get one tagline which will be meaningful to them. You simply must spend a few minutes informally mingling and engaging with them before you go up to take the podium. The skilful speaker is one who retains audience attention. A newspaper headline or a cartoon strip on a slide will keep the listener engaged while subtly making a point. Another good technique is to work in a quiz of some kind. Be prepared to answer some questions yourself if audiences don't respond. Most of all—rehearse. Be thorough about the subject on hand.

SHH . . .

You need to take some precautions. Insist that all cellphones are switched off near the microphone. A cellphone in the 'Silent' mode is not silent for the audio system. Here is a magical truth: the world will still manage to spin while your cellphone is switched off.

THINK ON YOUR FEET

Lastly, learn to turn every opportunity into an advantage. At a recent seminar, I was impressed with the way the guest who spoke last began his address: 'I have the advantage of being the last speaker . . . I can now echo the message of the speakers before me . . .' I thought it was perfect!

To sum up: be confident, clear and concise, use crisp visuals and ensure audience participation to have people hanging on to your every word. Speak with the same ease as you would if you were talking to four of your best friends—that tone appeals to all!

2

THE MOBILE AND THE MOUSE

Shouting and Other Email Faux Pas

There're grammar and manners to be followed in cyber space too!

The other day I received the following email from a client's office in response to a request I had made for some information:

WE WILL SEND THE INFO BY 2MRW EVE

FYI

NXT MEET PREPONED ON 12

HOPE U R FREE 2 ATTND

RGDS

XYZ

Looking at it I realized that our young and 'with it' population, one of our greatest assets, needs to polish its email etiquette.

My guess is that several readers of this email will find nothing wrong with it. There probably would not be anything very wrong had it been sent as a casual communication between friends. But in a business scenario it is all wrong.

CAPITAL MISTAKES

First things first. Look at the font. The entire message is typed in capital letters. In the world of emails, that amounts to shouting. A Westerner receiving such a mail would jump to the conclusion that the sender is very angry or irritated with him/her, and is not bothering to hide the fact. James, one of my newer clients, took offence when one of my colleagues wrote in the subject line 'RESENDING' in caps. He told her politely that she needed to stay cool! Needless to say, the Indian correspondent was not being rude but was merely using the 'All Caps' option for ease of typing.

So please take care to press the 'Shift' key when you want to put in capital letters where grammar requires you to but otherwise stick to the lower case.

NO SHORT FRMS PLS

To get back to our sample email: You will notice several abbreviations. So what? you might ask. In an email, abbreviations such as '2mrw' and 'U R' are totally unprofessional and unacceptable. Treat business emails just as you would any other business correspondence. I don't even recommend this for SMS communication.

Remember you are making a lasting impression on people you may never meet in today's virtual world. This attention to detail is as important as a live meeting where women business managers would not want to appear with lipstick smudges on their teeth, or men with spinach stuck in them!

PUNCTUATION POINTS

There are also no punctuation marks in the email I have quoted. Perhaps the sender thought they were not necessary, considering it was 'only' an email. There are others who simply strew their emails with exclamation marks, question marks and even emoticons. Take this one, for example:

> 'Hello!!
>
> We have received the communication yesterday!!!!!!! Thanks!!!!!! Boss was happy. But one of the rods was bent in transit. What to do????'

Both extremes are unprofessional and create a bad impression not only about you but also about the company you represent.

MIND YOUR GRAMMAR

Grammar matters too. In the first email that I quoted, there are a couple of grammatical and semantic mistakes. See if you can spot them.

Whether you are dealing with expats or Indian colleagues, ensure that your communication is framed in correct, official language. Tighten the sentences and communicate clearly with as few and well chosen words as possible. A well written email earns you plus points in your readers' minds. Here are some general tips to follow while sending emails:

- *If you are unsure of how to address a person, stick to being formal.* Dear Mr/Ms X can't be wrong. If you don't know the gender, address the person by the full name, e.g. 'Dear Yasoshui Hanegawa' or 'Dear Jeanne Ranay'.
- *Be crisp*, concise and clear in your communication. Aside from an occasional friendly inquiry once you have established a level of comfort, keep to the point.
- *Format your email* so that the lines are well spaced and if you have to set down points, use bullets or even numbers. One email per subject gets attention and the one response that you need. Or one email with bulleted or numbered action items makes it easy for a decision maker to respond positively.
- *Do not put read or delivery receipts* giving the reader the task of pressing the button; instead, you could request them to acknowledge receipt of the email.
- *Limit attachments.* They clog the inbox and generally only serve to irritate recipients. Avoid them where possible.

- Where relevant, *preserve the email thread* so that the readers can follow the sequence of developments.
- *Don't hit the 'Reply All' button as a matter of course.* Think whether your reply to an email merits being sent to everyone who has been copied on it.
- *Use the 'CC' button judiciously.* The other day a colleague had to tell a co-worker that I, as CEO, need not be copied on every email communication between them, as it would only clutter my inbox and add unnecessarily to my load.
- *Use the 'Bcc' button* when you want to share the information with several people without sharing the private email contacts of the receivers. We had a South African client who wrote rather politely, asking that we continue to send him our Indian cultural programme announcements as he likes to hear from us but he didn't want his email publicized to others in the group. We should have been sensitive in the first place.
- *Check your email carefully for mistakes*, check that you have put what you want to convey in the clearest possible way, and only then press the 'Send' button. After a long proposal to a client, one of my colleagues was in for a rude shock as the client had no idea she was offering additional services for a fee. She had worded the proposal very well, he responded excited to do more with us but as she had not mentioned the word 'payment' clearly, he was in for a shock when she subsequently did. *The balance between nicety and clarity are slim but as necessary as water and oxygen to email life.*
- Finally, *be prompt with your correspondence.* The email is sent in the expectation of a quick response. Make sure that the expectation is met. Even if you cannot sort out the problem, acknowledge the email and let the sender know roughly when he or she should expect a response.

The drive and enthusiasm of the brave new generation is something the West envies. We also have the trump card of English knowledge which the East has less of. With a little polishing in e-etiquette, we could make the most of these advantages.

PS: The two mistakes to spot above were: 'Preponed' is not accepted English usage all over, though common in India; the correct word is 'Advanced'. Also, the email should have read 'advanced to 12th' instead of 'preponed on 12'.

Mind Your Cellphone Manners

A basic knowledge of etiquette in the unwired ether could earn you brownie points and land you that coveted business deal.

'We are taking on Western ways of change and progress without the responsibilities that go with it.' I first heard this refrain when we started driving cars other than Ambassadors and Fiats in India as we didn't use seat belts or observe traffic rules with our faster cars. I wonder if this 'rings' true again in the use of telecommunication equipment, specifically the mobile phone, which has made life at once easier and more challenging for managers.

One of the world's larger steel companies was moving expatriates to India. My team had rehearsed and geared up for the top official's visit. The Request for Proposal had gone well and they wanted to hire us. But (no) thanks to a colleague's ignorance of cellphone manners, we almost lost the business on his very first on-site visit. The Dutchman was visibly annoyed at how many times my colleague answered his cellphone and text messaged. He had managed to cleverly nip in and out of our conversations, picking up the thread and saying all the right things all along. However, our potential client's sense of disquiet and mine of gloom (as I watched his body language) continued to mount. I was not able to give my colleague the heads up without the client observing. Eventually, I saved the day by sending him an SMS from my own cellphone—my hand hidden inside my purse punching away—saying 'switch off your phone'!

Here are some ways to increase our immunity to the cellphone and SMS disease.

GROW UP AND KEEP IT BRIEF

Ah, the choice of ringtones that tempt us. But don't use loud and annoying ones. A baby crying or a Bollywood beat doesn't say much about you or your professional image, and they destroy the peace of all those around. Keep your calls brief.

REDUCE AUDIO NUISANCE

Cellphone sales are soaring, and at present there's no limit in sight; we know that the largest number of those mobiles will be sold in India. We have to be proactive to reduce noise pollution. Do switch off, or put in 'Silent' or 'Vibrate' mode phones at the work spot, meetings, conferences and public places such as theatres and restaurants. If and when you must speak, do so in quiet tones. *When you can't hear, don't raise your voice; raise your body instead and move out.* Where you can't, such as in a car, first seek permission to speak, then cover your phone with a cupped hand and speak into the microphone.

MAINTAIN EYE CONTACT

In meeting etiquette, the most important thing is to maintain eye contact to display your involvement with the topic at hand. This is something we as Indians are still learning to do. But all is lost when we check or respond to a text message, even if we have kept the phone silent. Never do this in a meeting.

It makes others feel you don't care about them. In the rare event of an emergency like an illness in your family where you are expecting a message, seek permission beforehand: 'I have a sick mother in hospital and may need to take a call.' Then you can keep your cellphone in 'Vibrate' mode.

LANGUAGE, LINGO, LNGAGE?

Because of the ease of sending text messages, we tend to neglect other people's needs. However, technology is not the issue—people are. I learnt all about SMS manners from my Finnish clients, past masters at telecom. Who better than the chief of Nokia to teach me about SMS etiquette? He led by example, treating it the same as any other business correspondence.

Here is an SMS sample from Jukka Lehtela, erstwhile chief of Nokia's India operations: Dear Ranjini, Request a delay in our meeting by 30 minutes. Brgds, Jukka.

Please notice the following seven things and see how many of these you would have done: Dear; name of the recipient; a comma after the recipient's name; capital 'R' for request as the first word of a message; full stop after sentence; salutation short form for 'Best Regards'; and the sender's name.

He always used a proper salutation and my name, and this touched me. I had Jukka's phone number saved and would have known the message was from him, but he always signed his name anyway. He did not allow himself any bizarre SMS language shortcuts and he used punctuation. Best of all, he—without exception—promptly acknowledged any SMS I sent him.

RETURN CALLS

OK, so you did all the above, kept your phone silent and did not respond to text messages during a meeting. But now you have folks who tried to reach you. Well, return every call—you must.

A senior vice-president of Ford Motors taught me this. He was in the midst of some business one morning, when I called his cellphone and he said he would call me back. That evening he called me on his drive home from the factory apologizing profusely, as I would have done only if I had committed a grave error. He explained himself and how it was his policy to return calls within four hours. 'Gosh, if he can return every call he receives while he manages one of the world's largest auto manufacturing facilities, I jolly well should be able to do the same,' I thought.

SMS IN LIEU OF CALLS

When I have a missed call, I also use an SMS apologizing and asking the person to send me a text message. This is less intrusive and allows me to save my time and theirs. When we ask the caller to SMS, usually the issue becomes shorter and more effective.

So, Global Indians, do help yourself and others the next time you launch into the unwired ether.

3

PLAN TO WIN

Workplace Strategies

Looking at yourself through an expatriate's eyes can be a real eye-opener.

I thought I'd share with you an email I received a while back from an expatriate manager in a leading global car manufacturing company. Paul wrote the lines below and I feel it may be an eye-opener for Gobal Indian managers as to what an American boss may think of his Indian team.

> My 2-plus years in India were filled with many pleasant surprises and naturally some negatives. I consider myself well travelled and have experienced different cultures in various regions of the world. India was unique, in particular the business related experience I gained and learned from our host employees.
>
> We arrived with the mindset that our engineers in the US have designed and developed this state-of-the-art machinery that is designed for labour-intensive environments where the concepts of lean manufacturing can be best utilised. To my pleasant surprise, when I shared the prints with our freshly hired engineers to review what they were about to receive in the various sea containers heading our way from Italy, the US and other parts of the world, their dedication and enthusiasm immediately bloomed.
>
> They, after continuously checking with me for permission (a big cultural difference), redesigned the whole floor layout and some of the equipment too, to better suit the local environment.

At the first run, and without seeing the actual machines, they were able to reduce the floor space it was to occupy by about 50 per cent. The bottom line—the equipment, though designed with a 'lean' mentality in the US, was extremely 'fat', full of 'waste' in the local eye. The negative consequence of that was safety. Many could or would not see the reason for many of the safety features built into the machines to protect the worker from injury or in some cases death.

It took some time to have the local engineers be self-driven and make their own decisions. They were used to getting their bosses' permission before every step. Once they got used to being self-directed, they simply flourished. The culture can do so much with a whole lot less. Inefficient in many ways, yet extremely resourceful like I have never seen anywhere.

Insight for Outsiders:

Delegate and rule.

Giving Indian team members the authority and direction and then refusing to continue to hold their hands has to be a proactive strategy adapted by Westerners working in India. Otherwise this patriarchal approach towards a boss will end up in them checking with you every step of the way. Goal setting doesn't come naturally in the Indian management style, and helping with this is still a good idea for short and long term goals.

Here are two main areas to focus on to become self-directed as Paul calls it.

BUILD YOUR SELF-CONFIDENCE

There are three ways to do this:

- *Focus on your strengths, not on your weaknesses*: 'Give yourself permission to be imperfect,' as an American client

Sherry Murphree once told me. It is good enough if some of the people like you some of the time. Concentrate on the things you know you are good at; write down as many things about yourself that you can think of, which are strengths, and pat yourself on the back.

- *Remember your past successes*: If you have succeeded in something before, there is no reason why you won't in this new task too. Imagine yourself succeeding and then proceed full throttle; it helps you succeed again.
- *Court risk*: It is always a challenge to do something new but try it—you can't lose. You can only take away a life lesson. So when you have to try something for the first time, go for it and imagine yourself succeeding, use self talk and see your potential swell.

PRIORITIZE YOUR TIME

While time management is seemingly a bottomless pit to explore, there is a simple way to prioritize your tasks—take a task on first if the response to any of the following questions is a 'yes':

- Are other people depending on you to complete a task, especially if it is a component of an important project, and can a small amount of your effort go a long way?
- Is the value or profitability of the job at hand very high?
- Is your boss repeatedly requesting, nay pressuring, you to complete a legitimate job?

With self-confidence and prioritization of tasks you will already have won half the battle, unlike someone who does not take the initiative and seems inefficient. You will be able to transform yourself into a self-directed person, going to a boss only after really trying your own steps out. At that time, perhaps, do set deadlines collaboratively.

Spend some time introspecting each day. Did you do better than yesterday? Did you complete the task on time? Did you go for approvals to your team and lead less than in the previous project? Keep these scores for yourself in your little reference notebook; you can witness your own progress this way.

The next Peter or Paul who works with you from overseas will have to change his tune to 'my India team is efficient AND resourceful.'

Plan Meetings with a GAP

Some practical tips to keeping your business meetings focused and productive.

As managers, we all need to apply learning to our work life so often. GAP is a terrific formula to conduct successful meetings. An American of Indian origin told me about it and I'm sharing it with you here. My immediate question when someone asks for a meeting now is: 'What's the GAP?' Setting the GAP, together with marking a clear start and end time, is a superb tool for productive meetings.

So here's what GAP means:

G—The Goal. When you call a meeting, clearly define the goal or purpose of the meeting. Long inconclusive meetings that reach nowhere leave you feeling rather wasted. All the time you are thinking of the emails, cellphone calls and, of course, text messages that are piling up. Is the goal to arrive at a decision, have a review of the past week or to plan a specific project? Put it down in writing so that during the meeting, planning and progress, this receives top-of-mind recall.

A—The Agenda. Even if the goal is clear, it is all too easy to speak of this, that and the other, and lose focus. Setting a clear, printed agenda and placing one in each attendee's hand keeps things on track. The chairperson should also see to it that off-agenda topics don't take over meetings—he should bring people gently but firmly back to the discussion points. During a recent meeting, the chairing officer was often heard saying 'This is a process review challenges listing meeting; we will have another one for solutions.' He then drew up a new GAP for the solutions part at meeting two.

P—The Preparation. What does the person planning the meet have to come prepared with? Is there, perhaps, a report he needs to read or do some number crunching beforehand? Could one of the participants do a comparative study? Can someone else check a website or two for added information that would help the meeting? Should everyone be brushing up on a specific topic under discussion? For example, during a recent HR issues meeting in our team, we had everyone reread our HR induction process manual as a reminder. We started our meeting with a show of hands of those who had read it, not when they joined but in the week before the meeting. Public accountability is great motivation and makes us perform! It sure keeps me on my toes.

This brings to mind a series of meetings I had with some people. In the course of various meetings, I had noticed some things which worked with them and some which didn't. Here are three taboos in body language I observed during those meetings. Do these or similar ones apply to you? Ask a colleague after you read this list to find out. Get conscious of it and chuck the habit early to be more effective:

- *Eye contact*: Do you tend to look away or down mostly, avoiding the speaker's eyes during a meeting? It shows your disinterest even if that is not your intention.
- *Knuckle breaking*: Do you crack your finger joints unconsciously? It may signal you are nervous when you are actually very relaxed and confident.

- *Pen clicking*: Do you tend to click the back of your pen rhythmically? It may send the message that you are fidgety and unfocused, while the truth maybe that you are super engaged.

Do the following five things, instead, to get the best out of the meeting and also to be someone whom others think it is a pleasure to meet with:

- *Answer to the point*. Long and verbose speech, pauses and not getting to the point soon enough make it hard for the listener's patience and actually show that you did not do the 'P' or preparation part of GAP very well.
- *Stay on track* and avoid getting entangled in too many details of a topic. For example, it is so easy to let technical details take over discussions at a meeting.
- If there are ten people in the meeting, ask yourself—*are all concerned interested in this level of discussion* or could you hold a one-on-one offline with one or two people which will be far more effective?
- *Practise active listening*. How do you do this? Take notes, nod often, smile—that shows true participation.
- *Ask intelligent questions* or make additional comments where appropriate; by making a note, asking for your interruption to be excused and then saying it briefly. An initial practice tip is to write out the point as you take notes, so you say it crisply and clearly. Otherwise it will be like the man who was likened to a bull's head—he had a point here and a point there and a lot of bull in between. Efficient meetings are non-negotiable in today's fast-paced flattened world.

PART 4

Personnel Tips

'People can only live fully by helping others to live. Cultures can only realize their further richness by honoring other traditions. And only by respecting natural life can humanity continue to exist.'

—Daisaku Ikeda, Japanese peace activist
and Buddhist leader

This section is about giving and receiving respect. What to you as an Indian is respectful, like the use of a word 'ji' as a suffix to a name, is not even understood in another culture. When you go to visit someone's office you may find being offered food or drink is a token of respect but a Westerner may find that exactly the opposite: 'I told her I don't want coffee or tea or juice or water, why does she insist?' is a common reaction Westerners have to the Indian refusal to take 'no' for an answer when we press refreshments on guests.

On the other hand camaraderie to a Westerner is offering to buy you a pint in the pub after work hours, which may not seem very respectful to you. Learning each other's ways is crucial to participating in the dance of IU—Intercultural Understanding.

Insight for Outsiders:

To Sir, with respect

Indians feel respected if you call them 'Sir' or 'Ma'am', they stand when elders enter a room, give gifts made of pure silver to show they value someone, pick and drop off a special guest in a chauffeur-driven car, and serve them a table full of multiple dishes to show they care. None of this may matter to an expatriate but trying any of this with a decision-maker on the Indian side is sure to earn brownie points.

Minimum please and thank you courtesies; standing at the correct distance from another person; letting people go out of an elevator before rushing in; being careful not to interrupt—these are a few things which work across the board and are seen as respectful universally if you are working in the global village we inhabit.

The articles from real-life situations shared here work wonders in giving and receiving respect to and from your customers by saying more or even less. Read on to explore for yourself.

1

KISS AND TELL

Keep It Simple and Straightforward

Simplicity and clarity are key to effective cross-cultural communication.

A manager I know wrote to an expatriate client: 'The agreement is attached for your perusal and signature. Quality is sustainable only when you have a long-term contract with the same client. Let's hope this fructifies quickly!'

Nothing wrong with this on the face of it. But as I told him later the business world overseas is really into simple words and, perhaps, it would have got across better if he had replaced 'for your perusal' with 'for you to go over' and 'hope this fructifies' with 'hope this happens'.

DON'T MAKE PEOPLE REACH FOR THEIR DICTIONARIES

From years of experience of working with clients from various nationalities and with constant inputs/corrections from a sister who's a 'naturalized' American, I can say that when it's all about communication, it's best to keep it simple. Our efforts to sound 'official' and 'correct' often go awry and just end up confusing the recipient.

DON'T GET CAUGHT OUT WITH CATCHPHRASES

Further, we Indians have a habit of picking up catchphrases from the West and using them liberally in conversation and written communication. Unfortunately, we forget that we need to be steeped in the social, political and cultural nuances of another country before we can use the idiomatic language of that country appropriately. In other words, when we use phrases and expressions from the West that catch our fancy, we often don't use them in the correct context and so inadvertently cause much merriment among our friends from outside India!

Also, we often only hear the phrases and don't see them written down, so chances are that we assume some things incorrectly. I have found myself red-faced on a couple of occasions. Take the time an American client used the expression 'when the rubber hits the road' meaning 'practical and hands on'. But hearing it as rubble and associating the phrase with the rubble that is used to lay roads, I convinced myself that the expression was 'when the rubble hits the road'. I used it happily and only when I saw some grins going around the room did I discover that it was a reference to the tyre (rubber) on the road! On another occasion a client referred to 'getting down to the wire' and I nodded sagely, thinking he was talking of some electrical project going on in his house, when he was really referring to a deadline that had to be met. My mistake!

If you hear a phrase that is unfamiliar, ask the user to explain it instead of guessing at both the words and their meaning. Then you'll be sure of using it correctly yourself.

BE 'WITH IT', NOT OUTDATED

'Cool', 'hot', 'rocking', 'awesome': these are bits of Western lingo which we have now made our own. But ensure that you use the correct terms. Remember, they change faster than the seasons.

Some young friends of mine were recently talking of a film actor as 'hot', when an older person commented that 'cool' had been the popular expression just a short time earlier. The youngsters replied that 'cool' was out and 'hot' was in. At this, a precocious pre-teen who was trying to be part of the group wanted to know if, by and by, the correct usage would be 'lukewarm'! Jokes apart, the point is valid—popular lingo is easily dated and if you use it, make sure you are in tune with the times.

THE PITFALLS OF 'INGLISH'

Another hurdle is 'Indianisms' that we take for granted in normal communication with our compatriots. 'Going out of station' is a well understood phrase here but Westerners would know it as 'out of town'. Asking a person for his 'good name' could be puzzling to a foreigner (he probably thinks all his names are good actually!). Inquiries regarding his 'family' when the questioner actually means 'wife' is not easy for him to understand. Also, the tendency to end a comment with the word 'no' is very common here; you often hear people say something like 'It's very hot, no?' The Indian will correctly interpret this to be an invitation to agree with the comment, as it is just a poor translation from the vernacular, but most expatriates wouldn't know what to make of it (I have heard them say 'It is very hot, yes' as a response!). The correct usage would be 'It's very hot, isn't it?'

The Indian tendency to use acronyms liberally is usually terribly confusing to the foreigner. As a country, we seem to have a special talent for reducing organizations, names and classifications to a set of letters. To us things like NRI, FDI, TRAI, BSNL, TN, UP and ISRO* are familiar, everyday terms. But to a foreigner they sound like codes and make communication very

*NRI: Non-Resident Indian, FDI: Foreign Direct Investment, TRAI: Telecommunication Regulatory Authority of India, BSNL: Bharat Sanchar Nigam Ltd, TN: Tamil Nadu, UP: Uttar Pradesh and ISRO: Indian Space Research Organisation.

difficult. Even AC is not easily interpreted as air-conditioner by the visitor as many of them don't need it in their colder climates. My advice would be to drop the use of acronyms when communicating with them.

In short, Keep It Simple and Straightforward, Global Indians.

The Power of Persuasion

A good manager is able to nudge people into doing what he or she wants them to do.

People skills are important in any situation. From convincing a sleepy four-year-old to drink a cup of milk before the school van arrives to persuading a sceptical overseas client that you have what it takes to achieve the targets and standards he has set, it's all about technique.

In the global scenario, the modern manager gets to deal with all kinds—the know-it-all, the doubter, the cautious, the prejudiced and the simply ignorant, to name a few. But the good manager is able to change his style like a chameleon and nudge people, whatever their nature or stance, into doing what he or she wants them to do.

In this article, I will illustrate some persuasion styles that work well universally.

KNOW YOUR CLIENTS

You need to know their special needs and their background. You will have to tailor your product to suit them and highlight how they will benefit by what you have to offer.

Europeans like their rooms to be bright and well lit. Keeping this in mind, my realty manager told our clients from Denmark that we had shortlisted properties with ample light for them. This convinced them to work with us rather than with a street broker who does not understand the European mindset.

BE PREPARED

Sometimes you know your prospective client is going to be hard to convince. The people you are dealing with may have given you the impression that they consider you a 'lesser being'. Acquire as much information as you can about the subject. Then present your case intelligently, and counter their arguments one by one. Be sure of yourself. If you know you are right, don't let anyone browbeat you into saying you are wrong.

Some clients take a lot of convincing. Mere words and promises will not do. They need real-life examples of how things work. Be prepared to quote examples of how others have used your product/services and gained from it. Ask satisfied customers for testimonials and make these easily accessible.

When the world's largest cellphone charger manufacturer from Finland inquired about our event management services to launch their factory, we clinched the deal by showing them testimonials, numbers and photos of what we had done for a huge Finnish telecom major in the special economic zone they were co-located in. Finns, like Indians, are modest; so we handled it in our own modest style, and we won the account!

Still on the subject of preparation, be prepared to answer questions. Put yourself in your audience's shoes and try to predict how they would view what you are trying to sell. Anticipate their doubts and be prepared to allay these. If your target audience makes suggestions, take these on board. If the suggestions are viable say you'll work on it, and if they're not then politely explain why. A client once brushed aside the need for a tutorial lunch as part of our intercultural awareness and business skills building programme, saying the participants would manage to eat with fork and knife once they got to the US. We explained that learning from mistakes in familiar territory would boost their self-confidence but took the client's problem of organizing the logistics on board. Instead of organizing a formal meal, we reduced it to a buffet but we got in the fork and knife practice.

CHANGE PLACES WITH YOUR TARGET

Taking forward the point about putting yourself in your target's place, try to see yourself as your client would see you. Analyse your dressing style, your speech and your body language. What do they convey to a stranger who is trying to size you up and judge whether it would be good to do business with you? If you feel that there is scope for improvement, don't lose any time—polish your appearance by getting an image makeover from a professional salon, improve the way you speak by imitating those who you see doing it well and carry yourself slim (join that gym, avoid those carbs!) and tall, till you are sure that you effortlessly convey the impression you intend.

Another good technique is to use your client's name while persuading them. It strikes a personal chord. But first find out how they would like to be addressed. The Western way of doing business is more informal than the Indian one but it is always good to use their names. Also, use and imitate their speech and style. For instance, when I speak to Japanese people I use their slower tone with appropriate sighs and pauses, still doing it respectfully, without ever making it look like I am mocking them. People get convinced when we speak their language, literally or speed of speech-wise.

Last but not least, make yourself familiar with the hierarchy in your prospective client's set-up. Understand the scope of authority of the person or persons you are dealing with and judge when they have done as much as is possible. Quickly escalate the issue to the next stage, taking care that the original contacts do not lose face. I recently clinched a deal when a city head brought his boss—the regional head—to make a final decision of partnering with us on our website by directly asking the boss if he could 'truly' make a spot decision as his colleague had spoken so highly of his dynamism. He bought the space and everyone was happy.

To sum up clarity, confidence and courtesy are sure to win the day for you in persuading people!

When to Ask for More

Cues for avoiding social blunders

There are so many little niceties which make life's moments special but sometimes small acts in response seem to make for uncomfortable moments. The basis of etiquette is always to raise the comfort level of the other person and if we lived in awareness of this single principle, then we would not make too many blunders.

The other day a young colleague brought chocolate bars for her teammates to thank them for supporting her in a project. One of them asked her, 'Do I take one or two?' The question was innocently asked but caused a moment of fleeting awkwardness. Let's look at a simple, possible scenario: If one person were to take more than his or her intended share, there may not be enough chocolate bars for all the people on the team. This premise dictates that you don't ask that rather embarrassing question, doesn't it? Also, how could she say 'Please take just one and if there is more I will bring it back to you' without feeling like she was insulting the colleague who was only asking for an extra bar of chocolate?

I am often stunned at the lack of simple common sense where good manners are concerned. We can't act with a provincial mindset—not when India is in full view of the world, attracting billions of dollars in overseas funds and investments a week as newspaper reports say.

So it may be a good idea to look at a few occasions when it is OK to 'ask for more' and also to understand what to say, when to say it, how to say it and how much to say when you are asking for more:

- *Ask for more work* when you don't have enough to do or when your company has work that needs doing and not enough hands to do it. It will protect your job; even in tough times, no boss lays off his/her best and most willing worker who stretches himself/herself to full capacity.
- *Ask for more clarity* on a task when it is given to you. Emails and SMSs can be confusing and cross-checking to understand the task properly will provide you with efficient and timely task completion possibilities.
- *Ask for more money* when the cause is good but always affirm 'if the budget allows it'; whether right now or later, you will get what you deserve.
- *Ask for more advice* when you are not sure of what to do or how to do something. There are many experts right in your front yard; you simply have to recognize them. And as they say when you want money, if you ask for advice then money too comes automatically.
- *Ask for more food* when you really appreciate a dish but make sure there is enough for all first and then take a small second helping to ensure enough seconds for all.
- *Ask for more time* while working on a task by assessing the real hours or days it might take but especially when you know you won't be able to complete something you took on. Do it before the set deadline so that there are no unpleasant surprises from unexpected delays.
- *Ask for more help* to prioritize tasks when you have too much to juggle and can't really decide what needs to be done first. Ask for more help also when you can't do it by yourself. Seek additional resources or technical tools to speed up and improve efficiency. If you clearly show the

RoI (Return on Investment), people give you manpower or gadgets.

- *Ask for more information* on topics which are of interest to the other person (a sport, hobby, a recent trip); chances are they will enjoy telling you about it and the chat will help build interpersonal relations.
- *Ask for more authority* to take independent decisions. Also take the responsibility this brings, being aware that you will be subject to scrutiny—show you are a person of substance.

So to go back to the story of my young colleague who was thanking team members with chocolate bars, here are a few other responses I heard from her team members, which were a great match to the generosity of the original gesture:

- 'How kind of you to bring this to thank us.' (*Simply stating the obvious*)
- 'You didn't have to go to all this trouble but thank you.' (*Showing that it was an unexpected gesture*)
- 'I love Cadbury bars; always glad to help.' (*Including a specific comment in the thank you*)
- 'That looks delicious; it was a pleasure to be of assistance.' (*Commenting on the past and present, i.e., the project and the chocolate bar*)
- 'We always wish you well; good luck for the future too.' (*Building the relationship further*)

2

HIERARCHY HURDLES

Respect Transcends Cultures and Roles

Respect has different connotations in different parts of the world. Here's how to strike a working balance.

When you ask expatriates working with Indian teams how their interactions are, sometimes the answer is: 'It is difficult for us to really interact as there is a kind of wall; Indians are friendly but our "status" prevents interaction. In Denmark, society is as flat as a piece of paper; in Italy, it is less so than Denmark but not anywhere is it as hierarchical as in India. We feel respected if someone is critical and disagrees with us politely. Whereas Indians feel they are respecting us if they agree.'

KNOWING HOW TO RAP KNUCKLES

Reprimanding someone, especially in front of his superior, is an art in India as this story from an Indian company aptly illustrates:

Business owner: Why didn't you release this extra telephone line? You have been wasting company funds on this bill month after month when we aren't using it.

Ashok: Ma'am, you did not make up your mind. At times, you said you needed the old phone to have a forwarding facility to the new office so that we don't lose any business.

Business owner: Yes, but that was over a year and a half ago. Why did you not follow up since then?

Ashok: (*Looks at his superior Adit, who is also in the room within earshot, and raises his voice to defend himself.*): Ma'am, you don't know all the things I am doing, stretching myself always . . .

(*Seeing his look towards Adit and also noticing his crestfallen expression, the boss immediately changes her tactics.*)

Business owner: Ashok, it is a Rs 500-plan; I see that now. So you have at least reduced it from the Rs 999-plan that they had started with (*saving the employee's face*).

Ashok: Yes ma'am, I did that for all the phones when the plan prices dropped.

Business owner: I wish I had remembered to tell you to go ahead and cancel the extra phone line altogether. Anyway, do that now. And how is your new house coming along?

Ashok: We just moved in, (*smiles*) thanks ma'am for loaning me money for the down payment.

Business owner: It is all God's grace.

Notice how the personal and professional are mixed in the Indian workplace scenario. The boss has used her matriarchal role to go out of her way and finance money for the employee's home loan. She rewards his loyalty to the company by this gesture and hopes that this action would go on to increase his sense of loyalty. She is unhappy about his lack of initiative in the scenario where he could have surrendered an extra phone line but is quickly willing to overlook expenses that could have been controlled just to let him save face. The employee, on the other hand, is glad to have his family and home helped, and will waver between being polite and humble as well as prickly when admonished in front of his immediate supervisor. This game is like the one that we play in a family where each member is aware of how the other will react and adjusts his/her behaviour based on expectations.

Once again, the collective good of all is the core of corporate behaviour in India.

Insight for Outsiders:

Get personal in business.

Just being direct as a boss and sticking to work rules, with no attention paid to personal well-being, is not sustainable team behaviour in India. The need is to soften the blow of criticism. A boss is expected to be concerned and look after the well-being of the employee and his family. Include them in your conversation; you will get the loyalty of your staff which will translate into productivity too.

THE BIG BOSS

The boss is looked upon as a patriarch and is seen as a 'mother' or 'father' to the employee.

Who is a good boss? In India a good boss is one who looks after you (and your family), gives you generous sums of money, a good title and regular guidance on the work you do. In the West a good boss is one who serves as a role model, gives you a good salary, sufficient authority and provides you the space to perform—providing direction only if needed.

Who is a good employee? In India a good employee/subordinate is one who doesn't take too many vacations, is always ready to comply with the boss's requests and is honest. In the West a good employee is one who uses initiative and thinks for himself, who keeps to deadlines and always asks for clarifications where needed.

And who is a good colleague? In the Indian scenario a good colleague is one who is glad to help you in your tasks if you need his time, one who shares his space and personal as well as professional time with you. In the West, a good colleague is one who shares small bursts of break time amidst focused work spells in a day, and one who contributes ideas and communicates well in the professional sphere.

So the rule of thumb is to adapt to different management styles and working cultures depending on which team you are a part of—whether you are a boss, an employee or a colleague. Adjusting your behaviour to give and receive respect based on what the norm is for the other is the need of today's global citizen.

A Matter of Space

Clues to respecting another's personal space

I was at a party recently and felt distinctly uncomfortable during a conversation even though the person I was speaking to was someone I knew well. Suddenly, I realized what it was. The physical space between us was too close for my comfort. I took a step back to balance it out and get comfortable again but the person stepped forward to fill it once more! Then, I stepped back further and the person moved forward and the game continued . . .

In England there is a saying: 'I am the letter 'D' and this (the curve in front) is my space. You are another letter D facing me and that imaginary curve is your space. We both have to hold conversations without invading each other's space and then we will be comfortable.'

If we don't observe correct spatial behaviour in different cultures, it is distracting enough to prevent communication. Let's look at some key areas.

ELEVATOR

In the elevator (or lift, as we call it in India), everyone observes the same routine in most countries. They face the front and look at the display of floors as they light up above the door. It would be rude to stare, instead, at someone else's dress or papers be it a man or a woman. It is taboo to face the other way around and hold a conversation while riding with someone you know, to respect others' elevator space. So the spatial rule for elevators is—grow slimmer and taller as more and more people come into the lift. If you make eye contact smile briefly, and when you need to exit before others, say 'excuse me' and step out. Always let people get off an elevator before you get on. Always go up on tiptoe to let them go past you if they get off on a floor before yours, or even step out to let them out and then step back in. Stay silent, preferably (it is just a few seconds after all), or speak in low tones if you must.

CONVERSATION

In the Western world, the 'D' space translates into staying at handshaking distance of the other person. In Japan, move further away and stay at bowing distance, maintaining this space throughout the conversation. In the Arab world, don't be surprised if they stand really close to you. It is OK in that culture as they hug to greet each other, remember? General rule in India—stand about two feet away.

DINING

When you are at a table and sitting close together, it is best to watch where you place your arms. The rule when there is food on the table goes like this: 'Wrists—always, forearms—sometimes, elbows—never.' This simply gives more room for all diners and makes dining an enjoyable experience. Don't place any of your gadgets such as cellphones, or keys and bags on the table cluttering space; place them by your leg, on your lap or on the back of your chair.

All observance of spatial behaviour is part of an important life practice—putting others first. It makes you a better human being.

It's the Little Touches That Matter

A word of appreciation, an open mind, a thoughtful gesture—simple but effective ways of telling colleagues they count.

What does it take to be a good manager? Besides a B-school education, well honed systems and processes, strategic thinking and implementable action plans, your team will gel if you take the following four steps.

LISTEN TO YOUR COLLEAGUES

As symbolized by Ganesh with his large ears, a good manager must be listening all the time to pick up the early cues. Even if you are busy—leaving on an international trip or juggling multiple responsibilities, and there is a reporting manager who you know is handling her team well, step in for that twenty-minute chat or lend an ear to a colleague you know is hurting or confused. Ensure that the manager is present during the chat because your intention is to help her, not undermine her efforts or relationship. In niche small organizations people follow people, not ideas. So always ask yourself, are you someone you would follow? Then listen wholeheartedly to others.

Insight for Outsiders:

Big on Wisdom

Ganesh is the beloved elephant-headed god of India who is full of symbolism: the big ears are for listening twice as much as you speak, the trunk is for being able to discern just as an elephant does with a blade of grass or a boulder, the big stomach is for digesting whatever life has to offer and the broken tusk is acceptance of one's own faults. So Ganesh stands for many leadership qualities in life. He is best-known as the remover of obstacles.

OPEN YOUR MIND, NOT YOUR MOUTH

While the quality of one's speech is judged by the use of words, the quality of one's listening hinges on the lack of it. Don't claim to be listening and then rush in to talk, explain, draw parallels or try to offer solutions and suggestions. Be empathetic and let the person say what's on his or her mind, draw them out with encouraging phrases like 'Feel free to tell me what is bothering you; I know you say it is a bunch of small things, nothing big, but I want to hear them; I don't want you to feel burdened even by small things; your work is important to me and to our organization.'

VALUE ADD TO FAMILY

A good boss in India is one who cares about the welfare of the employees' families and cares enough to ask after them and theirs sincerely. A reliable boss is one whom the team member can turn to for assistance or guidance beyond the sphere of work. This bonding in Indian work relationships is now a Harvard study by Peter Capelli and his team. It is surprising that this is a topic of study because for the longest time 'we have been like that only'.

Strengthening this trait in today's fast-paced life is well worth it. Helping a long-term employee secure a seat for his/her child in a convent school if you can; giving an interest-free home loan to another longstanding performer; and offering flexi-hours and paperwork support to a key employee going through a difficult divorce: such gestures won't cost you FBT (Fringe

Benefit Tax) but they will yield FBL (Forever Bonded Loyalty) from key players. Look for ways to help others. What goes around comes around!

EXTEND APPRECIATION

Money and bonuses are a given and when more is made, more can be distributed. But going beyond the monetary aspect works magic. A personal note of appreciation to a colleague; a handpicked gift to suit the personality of a particular employee; or a spa or holiday gift or a luncheon with your personal time invested, will mean much more.

Indra Nooyi is an exemplary leader who goes out of her way in this regard. She would write end-of-the-year notes to spouses of her board members for their support through the year that had helped her colleagues work long and effective hours. But, as she says, her Indian upbringing made her reflect on another important aspect. When she was appointed CEO of Pepsi, friends would come to her home in Chennai and offer a quick word of congratulation to her but would spend much more time telling her mother how well she had done in raising her daughter and how much she was responsible for her success.

So Nooyi wrote personal notes thanking parents of her board members, and the response was overwhelmingly moving and lasting. Now, in the next phase, she spends a day with each parent, even flying as far as Mexico to be with one mother, booking a beauty parlour experience for them to enjoy together. She has seen tears of joy and acts of company loyalty grow side-by-side.

Nooyi's life is her message to us. It is so easy and simple to do, and so easy to forget to do too. L—Listening, O—Openness, V—Value-adding in the personal sphere and E—Extending appreciation: these are the four steps. And it spells LOVE. As the age-old saying goes, love is what makes the world go round.

A manager or top leader's attention to LOVE is the needed addition for corporate strategy, capability management modules or six sigma to truly succeed. It is enduring because, after all, to borrow from the seventeenth-century English poet John Donne, no boss is an island entire of himself. He needs his people to succeed at work. And LOVE matters to people.

3

CLIENT CALLING

Ironing out Cultural Differences

Strategies to deal with cross-cultural issues in the workplace

As India enters a new era of doing business with the world, the time has come to review our traditional people skills, take stock of what is good and what is not, discard the methods that have crossed their 'use by' date and bring new ones on board.

Here, I have put together a selection of the more common scenarios that managers face and how they could be handled.

WHEN CLIENTS SAY 'TRASH THE RED TAPE'

A pushy client/customer is a recurrent bane. Indians are used to being fobbed off by the rule book: 'This can't be done today. It has to be sent to the deputy tahsildar, the tahsildar next and then to the registrar for approval. Come next week.' More often than not, we don't even think of questioning the instruction.

But the Westerner, particularly the American, is used to getting things done now. Quote procedure to him, and he won't understand. So what do you do when someone from Company X's finance and accounting department calls asking for information that cannot be supplied without a fairly lengthy approval process? He refuses to accept that he has to wait and instead bombards you with a long list of reasons why the entire process needs to be bypassed.

Bruce: Hello, Anand. This is Bruce from X Finance. I urgently need document ABC from you. Can you send it across in two hours please?

Anand: Oh good morning Bruce. Please tell me exactly what you need?

Bruce: Document ABC which we used in project Y . . . It's imperative that I get it in two hours. The chairman is holding a review of the mid-year accounts sheets at 4 this evening.'

Anand: (*Listening noises and taking notes.*)

Bruce: I need to study the ABC document so that I can prepare an at-a-glance sheet for the chairman.

Anand: (*Still more listening noises.*)

(*In such a situation, Anand should hear Bruce out patiently and sympathetically. When he has finished giving all the reasons why he needs the ABC report pronto, Anand should take it forward this way.*)

Anand: Bruce, I do understand how crucial report ABC is to you.

(*This will automatically put Bruce in a good enough frame of mind to hear Anand out in his turn.*)

Anand: But I'm afraid it's going to be impossible to get the report to you in two hours. I will need to extract x, y and z data from various sources and I'll need to have our chief accounts officer's sanction for that. I will need to put up a paper to him explaining why I need access to these sources. After he satisfies himself, he will have to authorize software changes to enable me to access the information. This will probably need the CEO's sanction as well. So two hours is out of the question, you will understand . . .

(*Bruce will most likely interrupt to keep saying how urgently he needs the report and insist it reaches him in two hours but Anand should calmly reiterate that it can't be done.*)

(*While making soothing noises, Anand should quickly calculate the minimum time required to prepare the ABC report. He could add 50 per cent more to that figure to give Bruce a deadline.*)

Anand: Bruce, I'll see that the report reaches you by 5.30 p.m. your time. That's the soonest I can promise.

(*Then work flat out to complete it in the originally assessed time, say by 4 p.m., and surprise Bruce!*)

WHEN CLIENTS WANT YOU TO READ BETWEEN THE LINES

One of our trainees once posed this question to me: 'I get a call from a harried director of finance asking me to generate a complex financial report. But he's so busy that he gives me only sketchy details of what he wants. How do I handle this to everyone's satisfaction?' Well, first of all, stay calm and patient. Here's what the conversation should sound like:

Deepa: Thank you for calling, Mike. But I'll need some more information before I can get the report ready for you. Would you prefer a call or an email with questions, please?

(*The most important thing is to prepare questions that elicit the information you need. Write it down, all in one place. You won't help yourself or your director by sending multiple mails or making call after call asking for information in bits and pieces.*)

Director: Send me an email; that would work best, I'm just going into a meeting.

Deepa: Right, Mike, I'll mail you and send the report just as soon as I can.

Director: Thanks.

Deepa: Oh, and Mike, I'd appreciate it if you would do a quick spot check of the report to see that it's what you asked for, before distributing it. Of course I'll ensure that it's accurate; it's just that this is such short notice and there might be some parameter or control that I may have missed.

(*Assertiveness for the good of any project is what senior leaders don't mind at all.*)

WHEN CLIENTS THINK YOU'VE GOT A MAGIC LAMP

What if the required report needs considerable effort from a variety of people and involves, in your estimate, a good week's work but the director is demanding that he gets it in two days at the latest?

Extract as much information as you can about what exactly it is the director wants—aggregation, analysis, formatting—and realistically assess the effort/time required. Let the director know that you fully appreciate the urgency involved but politely explain to her the complexity of the procedure and just what has to be done to generate it.

Don't commit yourself to an unrealistic deadline. It's better to be upfront and say 'No' than say 'Yes' and not deliver.

Venkat: Sorry, Jenny, I can't get it to you by the 5th but I'm sure I can give you a user-ready product by the 12th.

(*Jenny's obviously not going to be pleased but you can lessen the blow this way.*)

Venkat: Here is a plan: I could give you a working draft by the 5th, a revision with your input by the 8th and a pre-final version by the 10th. Then on the 12th, we will deliver a final product. How does that sound?

(*Once the report is done to Jenny's satisfaction, don't hesitate to let her know politely that in future you'd appreciate sufficient notice for such complex work.*)

Venkat (*after accepting compliments graciously*): Thanks, Jenny. We at PQR take pride in doing good work. I had to pull several of my staff off other projects to get your work done on time. It was so complex that it needed many hands to complete it as quickly as we've done. I know this requirement of yours was totally unexpected but please do try to give us fair warning the next time you want something of this magnitude, so that I can plan ahead.

Procedures, time frames and complex tasks are routine issues that crop up in this day and age of virtual work. I hope the scenarios I have presented will help you cope easily with such situations in your working lives. The bottom line is: 'Be solution-oriented and commit only to what you can deliver.'

Communicating across Cultures

Don't get your (cultural) wires crossed. Here's how.

I'd now like to share with you a scenario we come across often while working with companies and teams to ensure they communicate effectively with overseas clients. Across industries, you will find yourself having to explain delays and deal with people saying Indians are never on time.

I'm going to take you through such a situation and show you how it can be handled easily, while ensuring that both sides get a fair deal. The more we practise such calls, the more 'Global Indian' in our mindset we become; so let's debrief together.

- *Preparation* is key; prepare a list of points that are likely to be raised during a conference call and use it to help you respond.

- A *progress report* on the subject of the call could be sent out to all participants in advance as well.

Right, let's get started then.

Devi: Hi, I'm the GRT analyst representing my team, based in Bangalore, India. We have with us on this call Bradley and Jessica from Miami, and Tim and Fritz from Michigan. Hello, everyone.

(*After initial greetings are over*)

Devi: This telecon is to flag the progress of the ABC project. Did everyone get the mail I sent out yesterday listing the progress?

Bradley: Got it, Devi. Actually, it set alarm bells ringing. We seem to be off target quite a bit.

Tim: Yes, I thought so too. The second stage should have been well under way by now but we seem to be still wrestling with Stage I.

Devi: Yes, we are behind but not by much.

Jessica: I think we need to really pick up speed here. The information to be generated in Stage II is vital for some reports I need to prepare and this delay is sure to have a cascading effect.

Devi: Jessica, I understand your concern. From our side, I would like to say that the delay was unavoidable because the parameters were changed at the last minute by the Miami office and the new ones required software changes. We hadn't budgeted for the time it took for the changes to be made.

Fritz: What changes were made?

Bradley: There were requests for some new reports which meant that the data needed to be analysed differently.

Tim: Who needed the reports?

Devi: Bradley, perhaps you could explain to Tim the changes requested? For now, I'm going to solve this by seeing how best my team can address the problems caused by the delay. As you can see, the reasons for the setback were beyond our control.

Tim: Fine.

Devi: Jessica, I could ask my team to generate the first few pages of the reports, which are not dependent on these changes, if you feel that would help

Jessica: Yes, I'd be glad to have at least those; they will help me to start my work.

Fritz: Devi, could you get reports L and R too? I need those urgently for some indices I'm working on.

Devi: I'll consult my team and get back to you, shall I Fritz?

Fritz: Could you send them in by Friday?

Devi: I can give you a definite date via email only after talking with my team but we'll give it our best shot.

Fritz: Thanks.

Devi: Bradley, I recommend a conference call involving the heads of all departments before we finalize our next project. That way we can avoid last-minute changes that cost us heavily in terms of time and effort.

Bradley: Yes, that's something we've all learnt from this experience.

Devi: So, my team and I will continue our work. Now that the software has been debugged, things should go faster. We'll give priority to generating the first few pages of the report and explore the possibility of pushing through L and R as well.

Jessica: Thanks.

Devi: Have a good day, everybody!

NOTICE

— how cleverly Devi managed to *coordinate the call.* She kept everyone on track, discussing how to recoup from the effects of the delay.
— she did not accept responsibility for the delay because it was really not the fault of her team. But she managed to *establish priorities* so that the effects of the delay could be minimized.
— she *boosted her team's image* as a professional, committed unit.

SO REMEMBER . . .

- *Prepare your* opening comments to be polite and to keep you in control of the call. For example, Devi says 'I understand your concern . . .'
- *Offer partial solutions* to quickly win the client on to your side. Devi says 'I could ask my team to generate the first few pages . . .'
- *Walk the talk.* Devi will certainly have to commit to a deadline by email, as she has promised to do.

And the team will have to stick to the deadline she sets, herself, this time. Only then will the client believe in her. Walking the talk is crucial to doing business virtually across borders.

In summary, just remember the word POW—Prepare, Offer partial solutions and Walk the talk.

A Blend of East and West

Communications should keep up with the times, adhering to the old values while accommodating the demands of the day.

Dr Charles Savage, president and mentor, Knowledge Era Enterprises, is someone I work with on a fairly regular basis on various projects. Interactions with Dr Charles, as he likes to be called, always provide food for thought and point one in new directions. I thought I'd share with you a couple of insights gained from him in the course of our work on a programme for MBA students having Indian roots while flying high on global wings. Dr Charles has strong views on the matter of respect and reverence for elders/authority, which he shared with his students and me.

Here's what started our discussion on the subject. One of his students wrote to him:

> Sir Charles,
>
> I would like to ask you whether I should address you as Sir Charles or Dr Savage or Dr Charles Savage . . .
>
> I know this question may be a bit stupid but in the Indian culture we believe in giving respect to our elders, and out of immense respect for you, I address you as Sir.

Here's Dr Charles's reply:

> Dear Shashank,
>
> As you will have seen, I want to both honour your culture of deep respect for elders AND help you be open to adjusting this for work in other parts of the world.
>
> In companies, your 'elders' might not 'always be right'. They might not have understood the larger picture . . . And they might be corrupt.
>
> As a professional, I would expect you not to 'bow down' to an elder person in the company but be ready to 'lead from behind', to 'push back' and to ask 'powerful questions' that will ultimately help everyone.
>
> Of course, if you are 'curious', 'humble' and have 'courage' it comes more naturally, does it not?
>
> In other words, I'd like you to find your own inner strength so you can stand tall and be counted in all situations.
>
> So, my preference would be for you all to simply use Dr Charles.

Interesting, isn't it?

LEADING FROM BEHIND

As new managers, we should be mindful of our traditions, our values. But we should also place them in the modern context and see how we can 'stand tall', as Dr Charles puts it, while being rooted in our core principles: the perfect mix for the Global Indian.

I like what he says about 'leading from behind', don't you? In the business context, we hear a lot about 'leading from the front'. But Dr Charles talks of a committed employee/team member who, though not yet a leader, takes his responsibilities seriously enough to point out flaws to his/her superiors, together with a viable alternative.

A junior content writer in our team in the cultural magazine *Culturama* once told us we were promoting too many Chennai events, while readers were looking for pan-Indian cultural content. It took courage as she was only three months old in the company but as the editor I took her seriously and today she is managing editor of the magazine, touching expatriates and a growing population of Indian readers across the four metros!

When we, as managers, take 'ownership' of our roles we will find it impossible to sit back and say to ourselves, 'It's Madam's company, why should I bother to tell her this won't work? If this is the way she wants it done, who am I to say otherwise? When it falls flat, she won't be able to blame me.'

It takes courage to challenge a superior. It also takes tact. The trick is to be able to do it without being either disrespectful or threatening. That's where the humility which Dr Charles talks about has a role to play.

MOVING ON BUT STAYING ON TRACK

As Indians, we're taught that humility is a quality to be valued; we must not be pushy, overbearing or cocky. We need to respect our elders. That's fine but we also need to realize that the 'Yes Ma'am, No Ma'am, Three bags full Ma'am' era is on its way out. Modern heads of businesses are mostly enlightened enough to welcome constructive criticism from subordinates, if it leads to common good.

So it actually isn't a question of either/or when it comes to Indian culture versus Western, it's really more of a both/and situation, as Dr Charles himself put it. We should be able to move with the times while staying on our own, very solid track.

INTERDEPENDENCE IS THE KEY

Dr Charles favours a 'Co-creative Culture' where old assumptions that knowledge goes with age and older folk 'know it all', give place to a culture where openness, dialogue and discovery are encouraged. The Vedas, the Hindu holy books, take their name from the verb 'Vid' which means 'to know'. Just as one lifetime isn't enough to read and even mildly assimilate the Vedas, knowledge acquisition is an ongoing process in a person's life. An older person such as I has to be open to discovery and dialogue with twenty-somethings because they know so much more about modern gadgets and technology. They, in turn, can dialogue with experienced seniors about topics such as India and global awareness.

Insight for Outsiders:

'Respected Sir'

Guru in India means a teacher, usually of spirituality, but the term has also now come to mean mentor. 'Gu' means darkness and 'ru' means to remove. So a guru is one who removes the darkness of ignorance by shedding the light of knowledge. Indians prefer to have gurus treated with respect, and don't use the term in a flippant way at all.

INDIAN TRADITION + WESTERN STYLE

Of course, it makes it easier if team members do the challenging tactfully. A mid-manager in a Fortune 500 company read through a document framed by the vice-president (VP) and noticed that service tax escalation was not provided for in the contract. He sent it back, asking a question on a Post-It. The VP took note, made the change and, when the CEO complimented her on the effective contract, mentioned what a valuable player her team member had been. So, in the Western style, this manager proactively suggested a change in the document checked by a senior for the greater good of the company. But he did it the Indian way—without challenging the VP's authority in her face. This melding of styles is best for the New India.

Put another way, it's about the 'it's up to me' attitude, combined with skilful communication and the ability to present one's view sincerely, without antagonizing or offending the listener.

PART 5

Generally Speaking

> 'No culture can live if it attempts to be exclusive.'—Mahatma Gandhi

From the southernmost tip of Africa to the spruced up Bangalore airport, things happen which remind me of Global Indian traits. Watching these places and the people in those places can teach us, if we have powers of observation.

Leaders can teach us through their own life examples. I also have woven thoughts gathered from interactions with a wide range of teachers 'who could affect eternity' with lessons ranging from values to behaviours to learn and undo. The most successful Global Indians are an amazing mix of tradition and modernity. One specific person I met was Ravi Venkatesan, former chairman, Microsoft India. He is the most amazing leader, bright and compassionate at the same time. He chants the *Shiva Rudram* just as effortlessly and with as much commitment as he addresses thousands of the best IT minds. 'Grow the bottom-line along with the Emotional Quotient,' he would say.

This section will share thoughts on Dharmic values and behavioural skills expounded by Swamis and CEO Coaches. I hope the tips they teach stay with you.

1

INSPIRATIONS

An American Guru Inspires Behaviour Change

Actions and reactions have a bearing on how things pan out. If you're savvy about what works and what doesn't, you're on a winning streak.

I have had the privilege of being in a coaching session by Marshall Goldsmith who has been rated as 'perhaps the greatest teacher of leadership on the planet'. He says that people who are already successful are there because they are intelligent and skilful; all that stops them from reaching the next level is usually some irritating interpersonal behaviour and once this is addressed and changed, their success is bound to multiply. Marshall has helped many global leaders overcome annoying habits.

His book *What Got You Here Won't Get You There* sums up his philosophy. Do visit his website and read his book to truly benefit. I share a few behaviours to change we applied from a list he gives. In his inimitable humorous style, Marshall calls the list 'A chamber of horrors of bad behaviour'.

ADDING TOO MUCH VALUE: WHY PUT YOUR TWO CENTS INTO EVERYTHING?

The other day one of my team members with experience in the

realty field came up with an idea of how to market a property we had on our database. I knew it was a good idea—putting an advertisement in a national daily—that he was suggesting. Instead of simply saying 'Thank you, it's a great idea. Please go ahead and ask me if you need help,' I found myself telling him which paper to advertise in and how to word the advertisement. Maybe I added 10 per cent value but I took away 50 per cent of his motivation because the idea was no longer his; it became mine. I am working hard on consciously reducing this tendency.

WINNING TOO MUCH: THE NEED TO WIN AT ALL TIMES AND AT ALL COSTS

One of my most promising former team members had a short-lived tenure with us. I had hired her at the senior manager level and had a clear career path for her to become vice-president. But an overwhelming need to always come out on top made her a poor leader, although her skills and knowledge of intercultural learning were way above anyone else's in the company. Finally, we had to let her go, purely on account of a behavioural trait.

PASSING JUDGEMENT: THE NEED TO RATE OTHERS AND MAKE COMPARISONS

Closely linked to adding value is the immediate comparison radar that goes up when we see something others have done. A simple acceptance of another's work style is needed, for example, in written documentation so long as there are no glaring errors. Everyone cannot have a uniform style or match our own. As the editor of a cultural magazine for expatriates, I have had to learn to let all styles coexist and resist the urge to take out a red pen for correction. As a result, the magazine has become richer with different voices speaking.

STARTING WITH 'NO', 'BUT' OR 'HOWEVER'

Excessive use of these negative qualifiers is a way of telling the world we are right and they are wrong. When someone gives us an idea or a plan, if our reaction starts with 'No, but . . .' it dampens their spirit. Each time we catch ourselves using these words, let's levy a Rs 10-'fine' on ourselves and contribute the money to a kitty so that some good cause gets rich at the cost of our behaviour change! We do this in our company

SPEAKING WHEN ANGRY: USING EMOTIONAL OUTBURSTS TO MANAGE OTHERS

A foreign client we once had learnt it the hard way when he spoke in raised decibels and showered angry words on a valuable Indian colleague. It ended in the colleague's resignation and no amount of cajoling could get the Indian to change his mind. Anger is temporary madness, as our Hindu scriptures say, and it is best to raise one's tolerance level instead of one's voice. A thoughtful 'one minute' reprimand as Kenneth Blanchard recommends is a good way, spoken after the wave of anger has passed.

WITHHOLDING INFORMATION SO THAT WE HAVE AN ADVANTAGE OVER OTHERS

As an entrepreneur, my biggest challenge is how to get cross-selling to happen between various departments that are flourishing individually. Keeping the bigger picture of the company above ourselves would banish withholding of information.

FAILING TO SAY THANK YOU: THE WORST FORM OF BAD MANNERS

Sometimes, the easiest things to do are also the easiest things not to do. When someone on our team does something worthy why not simply thank them? Write it out in the old-fashioned way on a card (Who can display an email or SMS on their refrigerator door?) saying, 'Thank you for the terrific report; I am glad to have you on my team,' goes a long way and gives pleasure to the receiver and giver!

As I read Marshall's list, I found myself thinking 'Oh yes, I do this and this and sometimes even this . . .' I have therefore narrowed the list down and picked one area to work on this quarter—and hope you will too! It works at the office and at home as I have been discovering.

An Indian Guru Shares Principles That De-stress

RIDE to success with these easy-to-remember points of action.

Globalization brings traders to India's shores who always ask us what it is that keeps Indians calm and happy and how we find the inner balance lacking in some other cultures. I was reminded of this during a recent talk I heard (available online at www.Vedantavidyarthisangha.org) by Swami Parmarthananda.

Today's budding Global Indians might do well to get a refresher programme on a stress-free work-life principle. This principle, called *karma yoga* in Sanskrit, seems out of bounds with modernism but can be remembered with the acronym RIDE. The basis of all action, according to our beliefs, should be dictated by one principle—proper action (that which is correct and ethical) with the proper attitude (actions are seen as an offering to a superior force and results are accepted as we do a holy blessing). So what are this proper action and proper attitude, and what is RIDE?

R—Reduce incorrect or unethical activity. Gradually reduce all non-value-based actions; those actions and responses in life which become obstacles to our emotional balance by remaining in our hearts. A simple rule is: 'I avoid doing what I don't want others to do to me. I watch my action and responses, identify and eliminate the inappropriate parts of thought, word and deed.' For example, 'If I don't want to be spoken to rudely, I don't speak rudely even to my office assistant who places the coffee cup on my desk each day.'

I—Increase dharmic or appropriate and correct actions: Here is a modern, non-ritualistic version of the *Pancha Maha Yagna* or daily practice of five responsibilities prescribed in the Hindu scriptures that could easily apply to our work days. We increase responsibility when we show:

- To the supreme: A respectful attitude towards the five elements (at work the non-pollution or conservation of air, wind, water, earth).
- To living creatures: Corporate tree planting campaigns, environment friendly recycling, supporting animal NGOs.
- To humanity: Any Corporate Social Responsibility to people causes, even simply being respectful of team members.
- To institutions: Supporting with time or money the various institutions that promote spiritual values and cultural learning.
- To elders: Show respect, give time and resources to senior citizens, starting with those at home and work, with every opportunity provided in our work life.

D—Dedicate all actions to a divine being who oversees the universe, so that there is a good balance of the material and spiritual in our life. Then step forward and do your best to win, compete and fight justly to give your maximum output.

E—Experience all results as a blessing and a lesson to improve. If and when we fail, get rid of the 'Why Me?' syndrome. Look for hidden messages and work on criticisms to improve performance; know there is no injustice in life. The most painful experiences often have the best hidden messages; people who have been given the 'pink slip' or let off from a job in the US have ended up as extremely successful entrepreneurs. When we succeed, we should share it with others, as no person is an island. Remember the team effort that allowed us, as a new manager, to succeed.

There are clear benefits to RIDE:

- *Self-esteem*: Being more outward looking, we become less 'me focused'. We become a contributor rather than a consumer and find meaning in our life and job. We see the bigger picture of the work we are doing and it replaces our low self-image and inferiority complex converting it to heightened self-esteem.
- *Serenity*: Calmness, confidence and cheerfulness increase with this mental training. It is not fatalistic; we do our very best and acknowledge that there is a contributory role we play that is vital.
- *Harmony*: At the micro level, our teammates and our family, and at the macro level the whole environment is maintained in harmony as we contribute to spread harmony.

Only in India do we have the wonderful teaching of s*anatana dharma* or the eternal values. Let us salute India and set forth to conquer the world.

2

ABOUT THIS, THAT AND THE OTHER

Blazing a Business Trail in India

Interesting insights into the tradition and modernity of business in India

Entrepreneurship is all about doing new things or doing the same things in a new way—blazing a trail, in other words. Some countries and cultures are traditionally more geared towards this than others. The US, for instance, has long had a reputation for innovations and inventions. Perhaps it has something to do with the pioneering spirit of the early settlers who came from England and mainland Europe in search of pastures new and green, and found that entrepreneurship was non-negotiable for survival.

Insight for Outsiders:

Cultural background of business in India—family ties

In India, entrepreneurship is, or has till recently been, the clear prerogative of certain communities that have for generations been steeped in business: the Baniyas of the north and the Chettiars of the south, for instance. These communities revel in starting new ventures; they have a highly developed eye for business opportunities, and know how to drive a hard bargain.

However, for the majority of Indians, business or entrepreneurship, is associated with risk and risk is not something most Indians go out to meet. The safety and security of a government job was preferable to the uncharted seas of private enterprise. Safety still gets top priority to a large extent.

Nevertheless the spirit of entrepreneurship or, shall we say, enterprise has entered India, though it is at the nascent stage. 'Entrepreneur' is said to have come from two Sanskrit words: 'Antar' meaning 'inner' and 'prerna' denoting 'inspiration'.

NOTHING SUCCEEDS LIKE SUCCESS

Success stories are receiving so much publicity that more and more youngsters are discovering in themselves the courage to break away from the mantra of steady incomes and assured pensions to explore new and exciting avenues.

To an aspiring Indian business tycoon, the names of Narayana Murthy and Nandan Nilekani are surely nothing short of iconic. Imitation, as they say, is the highest compliment you can be paid, and these two gentlemen have been flooded with compliments because Infosys has inspired countless attempts to achieve similar success.

Infosys may be one of the best-known success stories but it is by no means the only one. Offhand I can cite my own meeting with Mr Nilekani, who calls himself an accidental entrepreneur and encourages others to follow their dream, tenaciously holding on to change and innovation.

FAIR WINDS AHEAD

The modern-day Indian who gives a second thought to starting out as a businessperson is encouraged by two main factors: an economic climate that is favourable to enterprise, and the faith that the West reposes in India demonstrated by the business houses of repute as well as individual business adventurers who are flocking to trade with and in India.

CHINA AND INDIA—SPOT THE DIFFERENCES

Harvard Business School Professor Tarun Khanna's highly acclaimed book—*Billions of Entrepreneurs: How China and India are Reshaping Their Futures and Yours*—makes a comparative study of the factors acting as catalysts to the spirit of enterprise in both these countries that, the world acknowledges, are going to be the powers of the future. I was at the Harvard COOP—the Cooperative society and famous bookshop at Harvard—when I heard him speak and do his book signing:

> For the first time since the rise of the West, entrepreneurs in Asia can ignore New York and London almost entirely, and still build companies worth billions. The economic centre of gravity is moving toward the East.
>
> In some sense people in these societies are running faster than their rules and laws can keep up. So they are creating the rules as they go along.
>
> In recent times China's hard-power global expansion has been the result of premeditated and orchestrated state policy, while India's influence in the world has largely been achieved through soft power.
>
> India oozes soft power. In India's noisy political economy, creativity and the arts thrive.

Talking of soft power, here is my personal *ten-point checklist for success as an entrepreneur*:

1. *Communication*: Be clear, concise and kind internally and externally.
2. *Team building*: Pay attention to all players and enhance cohesiveness by leading from the front.

3. *Smooth interpersonal skills*: Use 'I need you to include me more in information' instead of 'You did not tell me' phrases while interacting.
4. *Composure under stress*: Don't react but weigh the situation and postpone emotional response.
5. *Handling ambiguity*: Be prepared to chop and change as per customer need.
6. *Seeing the big picture*: This talent allows you to fulfil your customer's latent needs.
7. *Patience*: This is a must for results, for performance, for new ventures to succeed.
8. *Writing skills*: This encompasses text messages and emails. All should be treated as business communications, whether instructional or inspirational.
9. *Empathy*: Feel for your customer and your teammates, success will follow.
10. *Global mindset*: Understand, strategize and act knowing yourself, knowing the other side and adapting as the situation demands.

CHANGING TIMES

The entrepreneurial landscape is definitely changing—away from a marked tendency to keep it all in the family, with business communities displaying unwillingness to trust outsiders, to a situation where talent and drive, not birth and upbringing, are the factors that determine like spirits who draw together to set up and run successful ventures. Relevant education is also a high priority area: witness the mushrooming of B-schools across the country.

Let's welcome the professionally qualified, ever-innovative, brave new business Indian.

3

IT'S ALL ABOUT ADJUSTING

You Are in Queue

Order and discipline are taken for granted in the West. They're virtues we need to consciously cultivate.

I found myself one day at the new, state-of-the-art Bengaluru International Airport. The one-hour drive to and from the city was not as bad as I was told it would be. I had left for the airport two hours ahead of the scheduled check-in time as people had warned me it could take very long to get here. So there I was, with an extra hour to take in the new airport.

What an achievement of India's globalization this new airport in Bangalore is! The glass and steel structure, which lets natural light pass through its undulating roof, is modern, airy and welcoming. An oversized Louis Vuitton suitcase welcomes you at the entrance—I have not seen this advertising campaign in London, New York, San Francisco or even in Paris, which is the home of Louis Vuitton fashion.

Once you enter the airport you could be in the most modern city in the world. I had to pinch myself and say, 'Am I really in India?' Once past security, shops and eateries abound attracting sales and whetting appetites. The choices are many: La Moda stores are filled with Tommy Hilfiger, Calvin Klein, Police and other designer labels. Shoppers Stop has a mini-mall in here! Food options range from a Barista to an Illy café! The 'Taste of India' fast food counter, people milling around in large numbers, the languages you hear wafting around you and, yes, of course, the queuing in the toilets are the only reminders that 'This is India; we are like that only.'

While speaking to an American client that Global Adjustments had helped relocate from Texas to Chennai, we heard her say that one of the most frustrating things she found about India was waiting in queues. I was surprised because I thought Westerners were used to queuing patiently. She said it was not the act of queuing but the method of doing it that puzzled and irritated her. Then, she took out a marker and drew a diagram on the board for me. Take for instance queues in front of restrooms at hotels or theatres. She found that she would be waiting at the restroom's entrance while people brushed past her, and people who came in after her used the toilet before she did! Soon, she became wise to the trick and joined the 'Brush past and stand wherever there is elbow room in front of whichever door you can get to' gang.

If India is going the global route, if we are modernizing our country and life, then we have to modernize our minds and take on the responsibility that comes with progress. When we drive fast cars, we have to wear seat belts. When we consume alcohol, we have to follow the 'no driving after' policy. Similarly, let's queue correctly at our modern facilities.

Here is a recap of some simple queuing rules. If you travel overseas this is non-negotiable behaviour for you to adopt or you will be tagged rude and India will get a black mark. If you stay in India, do help start this ripple effect of change by demonstrating queuing courtesies and etiquette through your own behaviour.

QUEUING RULES

Some rules of forming a queue:

- Form a single queue.

- Be aware of queues, people and situations around you at all times.
- Don't hang on to your cellphone and perform robotic actions of joining any old queue.
- Leave breathing space between each person in the queue.
- Don't touch or push those in front of you; if you do so by mistake, apologize.
- If you are not sure where the queue ends, ask: 'Were you here first?'
- Don't break a queue just because some poor guy looked away for a minute.

QUEUE BREAKING RULES

These are to be used in an emergency only! Please attempt this only in an exceptional situation. For example, I was going to miss my flight the other day and the queue at the Chennai airport security check looked like it was a single one. I had to remember the two A's:

- *A-sk* for permission
- *A-pologize*

Ask a few people, 'My flight takes off in twenty minutes, is yours as soon or may I please pass?' As you make your way to the top of the queue, utter 'sorry' all the time as you are inconveniencing all those who are waiting in the queue.

Patience is a wonderful Indian quality as we wait for the monsoon, the right government, the results of an examination . . . Let's demonstrate it while queuing too.

A Compass, an Anchor and a Telescope

How not to lose your bearings in the global village

Another day found me at the Cape of Good Hope. It is on the south-western tip of the African continent and the place where the Indian and Atlantic Oceans meet. As I remembered from high school geography lessons, this is the place that Vasco da Gama and Bartholomew circumnavigated to discover the brave new world! What tools did they use to keep their vessel on track to reach the desired goal? A compass, a telescope and an anchor, for sure.

Global Indian managers who travel the flattened world would also need:

- A *culture* compass
- A *values* anchor
- A *planning* telescope

WHIP OUT THAT CULTURE COMPASS

When we interact with someone, it is not with a person exactly like ourselves. In virtual teams, on conference calls and in long-distance strategic partnerships, the players are increasingly from different backgrounds and with a different upbringing. So a culture compass is needed to keep checking the direction we are taking and the personalities we are dealing with. Are they used to direct communication? Should we make our communication more blunt to be understood, as in the case of, say, a North American? Are they, on the contrary, used to more indirect and roundabout ways of talking and should we be interpreting their body language and unsaid words as in the case of, say, the Japanese.

At our Global Adjustments training workshops, I prescribe that we whip out this compass and keep an eye on it, and adapt and adjust our behaviour to be successful based on what we know of the other person's ways of interacting. The most important thing to keep in mind is that no culture is superior to another—the minor overt differences just need adapting to, according to the situation.

DROP THAT VALUES ANCHOR

It is equally essential to anchor ourselves firmly in the values we believe in. Adapting has to go hand-in-hand with rooting ourselves in our values. Dropping anchor whenever the wind is too strong to continue sailing is a perfect metaphor for our cross-border behaviour in business.

If our value system is relationship-oriented and we find that in the more fact-oriented countries too direct an approach ends up in people being tossed about recklessly, we can say, 'I need to stop here. This current is too strong and may take me the wrong way, a way that I am not comfortable taking.' Then, anchoring ourselves in our belief, we must communicate our needs to the other side and find a via media sooner rather than later.

At a recent 'global emerging leaders' workshop, a young Indian participant, Rajesh, told me how he felt insulted when his Western colleague bluntly told him off for interrupting, in front of his teammates. He sulked a bit, felt hurt and then realized the Westerner had no clue he had hurt him because he had treated him just as he would a person from his own country. He took the Westerner aside and explained: 'I will try to hold back my interruptions. But since it is a habit that is not frowned on as much in our country as in yours, if I do it again please call me aside and mention it. Don't tell me so bluntly in front of my team, as I lose face with them.'

It took a lot of courage to say this, but now they have worked out a code—the Westerner raises a Victory sign when Rajesh falls back into his habit of interrupting and immediately, Rajesh says, 'Oops, sorry' and they carry on, using humour, respect and self-direction.

None of this would have happened if they hadn't taken the anchor time to assess each other's values and needs—the one of saving face, the other of not interrupting.

EYES ON THE HORIZON

This third aspect is so important but so subtle that it could get lost. We feel like we are dealing with planning but can't seem to look beyond the all-encompassing things going on now. There are piles of emails to answer, calls and text messages to return, meetings to attend and to-do lists to complete.

Our inbox is never going to be empty. So it is wise to have a structure in our days and weeks to plan for the long-term. What balance do I need in areas such as money management, health and fitness, recreation, personal and professional mastery, business and career, primary relationships (spouse and children), family (siblings, parents), social networks (contacts), income now and quantum income (one-time income like a book royalty). These are all areas to set goals in; assess where you are in each and where you want to be in each. Then set goals: clear measurable goals and actions to be taken so the wheel of life turns smoothly.

In the global village, we need this far-sightedness to be effective today, while we work with a plan for tomorrow. I always remember Zig Ziglar, the master coach, who asks, 'Are you a wandering generality or a meaningful specific and how can you hit a target you cannot see?'

PART 6
Global Indian

'Preservation of one's own culture does not require contempt or disrespect for other cultures.'

—Cesar Chavez, Mexican-American civil rights activist

For an Indian to say 'I am quite bold' is like Sleepy or Doc saying 'I am the tallest of Snow White's seven dwarfs', so I can't claim that self-confidence comes naturally to most Indians. But this is a scalable skill and as we improve our self-esteem, our self-confidence, soars. This section shares inspirations from my own life and those of towering giants, which show that nothing keeps us from playing an assertive role in carving out our own future. The trick is to give equal importance to our own tradition, rooting ourselves in it as we develop global wings.

This section is about conversations with incredible people from Nilekani to Vishwanathan Anand, about how to build on integrity, discipline and hard work while all the time paying attention to details, to become global players. It's also about how to navigate the world as a Global Indian, be it in matters of food or work attitudes from a returning NRI's perspective.

1

INDIA AND THE WORLD

Brand India

A country that means different things to different people—views from the globe

I have often asked myself, what is India? That has naturally led to the question, what is India to others? What does India stand for to the many expatriates who live and work in our country? In the course of my work with the expatriate community in India, I have tried to find the answers to my own question through the questions that people from around the world have asked me, and those that they have not asked me.

I found that each one of us has an India within ourselves. We all choose to define our country in a certain way and our experiences are coloured by the meanings we paint. Here, I share with you views from leaders in their fields, from across the world. The Brand India that they describe should serve as inspiration.

> Brand India for me signifies the young and the youthful. Just like the youth have a shortage of resources which they make up with unparalleled ambition and capability to demonstrate, India too is in the same boat. Once we overcome this dearth, the economy will only surge ahead.
>
> —Sachin Saxena, head of Nokia India Operations

> Every global superpower has witnessed a transition from adolescence to maturity . . . Over the last few years, India has

been moving towards that transition . . . I have worked closely with India's new generation and they are confident about who they are . . . In my assessment, they have understood that they are the 'I' in India, and that each one of them is contributing to building brand India.

—Michael Boneham, president and managing director, Ford India (Ford was among the first auto manufacturers to set up shop post-liberalization; today they export cars to the world market from India.)

Surely India has arrived in the world scene as an economic power. India has been a great global citizen with an exceptional record in the area of non-proliferation. India is viewed as a stable, honest country that values integrity and is ready to play a role in the global arena, be it in nuclear non-proliferation or in promoting green tech or in being a responsible member of the WTO.

—Lakshmi Narayanan, vice-chairman, Cognizant Technologies (Cognizant has been voted among the 100 best small American companies and rang the Nasdaq bell remotely from India.)

Twenty-five years ago, I worked for an all-white PR firm where I was viewed as the exotic Indian. Today, at Mayfield, the majority of our Managing Directors are of Indian origin, we invest in India with an on-the-ground team and many of our US Portfolio Company Entrepreneurs are first- and second-generation Indian immigrants. Both professionally and personally, I wear my Indian heritage with pride and know that my daughters are growing up with the Indian advantage.

—Kamini Ramani, marketing director, Mayfield Fund, San Francisco (Person of Indian origin and leader in the Silicon Valley)

India, you play a role in saving us from destruction—the destruction of having forgotten who we are. But you can only help us by remembering who you are. Which is not Bollywood and cell phones. Martin Luther King said, 'I can only be what I ought to be if you are what you ought to be; and you can only be what you ought to be if I am what I ought to be.' Gandhiji called it 'swadeshi'.

—Michael Nagler,
professor, University of California, Berkeley
(Winner of the 2007 Jamnalal Bajaj International Award
for Promoting Gandhian Values outside India)

The term Brand India could in my opinion refer to India's cohesive and comprehensive social design, the potential to absorb and assimilate alien influences and the ability to maintain a certain meaningful continuity. *Apne sanskar mat bhulo!* Don't forget your own values!

—Dr Petra Vogler, Germany,
intercultural management expert

The term Brand India for me can be defined with one simple word, Diversity. Where else will you find a farmer driving his ox cart while speaking on his mobile phone? Or witness a Mercedes Benz having to stop for a shepherd leading his flock across the road? At the top of this diversity brand is the openness and warmth of the Indian people and their inherent respect for others, which I hope remains.

—Kenneth J. Lemay, US, speaking from Pune
(Business leader in the manufacturing sector)

In India, I found you can have an idea and make it come true because other people dare to believe in the idea too. For me,

> India is about the power of a story to change reality. India is about the power of individuals choosing to believe in a story so passionately (a story larger than themselves) that together they make it come true.
>
> —Lisa Heyolauff, Germany, founder–director, 'Going to School' (a creative non-profit media trust for children in India)

So after hearing all those thoughts, what is Brand India to me? The truth is that I don't know for sure yet. I don't know whether it is the country's culture, its people, its diversity or its traditions. I don't know whether it is its smile, its sorrow, its colours or its unshakeable spirit. What I do know is that it is my identity, my root, my balance. It is what defines me.

The Coconut Generation

Problems of the returning Indian manager can be dealt with if you combine sensitivity with directness.

I heard an interesting phrase recently which refers to NRIs as the coconut generation—brown from the outside and white inside! I mean no offence as I repeat it here, as I think the diaspora has made us proud the world over.

Is there perhaps a lesson here for us about interactions with this new category? As the world gets smaller and India booms, a new breed of bosses and managers is on the rise—the non-resident or returning Indian. During the course of my journey at Global Adjustments, journalists have often asked me about the NRIs among my clients and their readjustment problems. I have also often heard—in our industry of relocation, realty and expatriate services—the constant complaint: 'NRIs are harder customers than total foreigners moving to our shores!'

A dialogue I once had in the US made me wonder what that

perception may be due to. I called up an NRI (a person of Indian origin, who had lived in the US for twenty-five years and had left India twenty years ago), whose contact I had been given by a friend in India, to see if I could get some input on connections to be made in her area. The dialogue went like this:

> I: Hi! I am a friend of Ashok and Manju; they gave me your number as I am visiting New York. But I am not sure this is a good time to talk?
>
> NRI: Actually it is not, I am on my way to a meeting, but what is this about?
>
> I: Well, it was just to get some information from you; I do have time till Saturday. Would you know about xyz department in your university, for me to speak with someone?
>
> NRI: There is no department of that name. People are very busy here and you can't meet them in two minutes or even two days. Anyway, why don't you call me at 1 or 1.15?
>
> * * *
>
> I: Hello again, it is 1.15 and I am calling back but don't know if it is busy for you, please?
>
> NRI: We can talk. So how do you know Ashok? What do you do? How come you have been invited to this meeting in Harvard . . . There is no such department but maybe you can talk to Professor abc who can tell you more.
>
> I: OK, I will meet up with him in the University.
>
> NRI: As I said, we are very busy here in America—I know you are very busy in India too—we can't just drop everything to see you . . .

The conversation ended with the NRI offering to meet me at a later date but I never called back. Being busy is fine. Saying you are busy is also OK. But saying things like 'we can't just drop everything' or 'you can't expect to see someone in two minutes or two days' is not useful to anyone, is it?

I ran this whole conversation by a Caucasian-American woman friend with whom I had a dinner meeting that night. I asked her if it was I as an Indian who was being sensitive, and how she felt about the whole exchange. She clearly termed it an offensive exchange, and said there was no need to be so abrasive.

Being direct is a great thing to learn from the West—it is necessary for survival. But isn't being blunt bordering on hurtful? I wonder if we should thicken our skin or tighten our tongue. Both can't hurt.

Anyway here are a few things that Global Indian managers and returning Indian managers would do well to remember.

DON'T TAKE IT PERSONALLY

The person you are having trouble dealing with is most probably reacting to a situation and isn't doing it deliberately to hurt us—if they knew better they would have stopped short. The NRI is neither being demanding deliberately (he has become used to more organized Western ways) nor is the Indian deliberately ripping you off (she is managing under circumstances where everything is not under her control).

DO REALIZE THERE IS A BACKGROUND

There is a cause for each person's behaviour. You may not know or understand it always but just be aware there is one for sure which is responsible for behaviours.

SWITCH HATS

The need to be direct or explicit and the need to preserve relationships are both important for the NRI's survival; he could be wearing one or the other hat depending on the circumstance. The Indian too could see him simply as wearing the 'other' hat.

Look out for body language or stony silences. It is possible to avert faux pas and hurt this way. All this is simply a case of tuning in and being more mindful.

Woman Power—It's Inspiring

Women all over the world, who've made a mark in diverse careers, are eager to share their insights with India. So, Indian women managers, go for it!

The Cherie Blair Foundation conference, 'Women Mean Business', is on at Mumbai. The Who's Who of Women Power raise their voices in unison for inclusive growth and advancement of women and girls in India. The role models are all here. They tell their story straight. They are ready to give to India, and all that the rest of us have to do is ask and be willing to commit to hard work.

To get to the conference, we drive on the amazing 'sea-link' just a few minutes from Worli to Bandra and onward to the venue. Is this our own 'Golden Gate Bridge' which speeds India's journey to the golden era of the twenty-first century? Will this journey be sustainable as the 'India softpower story', as Shashi Tharoor called it in an inspiring speech at TED (Technology Entertainment and Design) India? It will be sustainable, so long as we think of people and planet along with profit, I tell myself.

But the warning signs loom on the Mumbai skyline from this sea link bridge itself—I try to peer through the pollution-created haze at the city that houses Asia's largest slum. No, it is not just the 'December fog', as my driver assures me it is. This is nature calling out for recognition that there's immediate and urgent work to be done, much more than changing a few light bulbs at home.

Anyway back to women power—Cherie Blair, wife of the former British prime minister Tony Blair, had promised to commit to Asian women and be a catalyst of change in India. Now she has galvanized us all to sit together, talk, listen, share and commit.

A TOP COP SPEAKS

Kiran Bedi, India's first woman IPS officer, stole the show with her dual attitude of 'Never say die' and 'It's all up to me'. 'If you move me out of Delhi because I move and shake up the police system, and put me in a prison office, I will shake things up there as well and win an international Magsaysay Award in the process. I will run the Tihar Jail as an ashram and bring lasting change with or without the nods of required approval,' was her take! She reminds us of a cartoon strip on the day she was transferred out of Tihar, which said 'the most dangerous criminal of Tihar is released'! Not fazed, she talked to us of the achievable dream of Navjyoti, the NGO she runs, and is clear that so long as she has health, she will commit to the betterment of India. Her commitment is to create a huge workforce of 'caregivers' from the talented pool of Indian women who have completed twelfth grade. They will be trained to look after old people and children. This will free other Indian women to work longer and more calmly. This, in turn, will help in reducing the alarming attrition rate of women in IT.

WOMEN OF SUBSTANCE

That was the story of one powerful woman leader, and the conference heard about many other commitments from different fields—Vandana Luthra of VLCC Wellness and Fitness Clinics, who encourages imitation of her profit share-ownership model of entrepreneurship; Ritu Kumar who is willing to co-create with others a revival of dying arts in India; Loomba Trust's Raj who disarmingly reveals that his inspiration for his commitment to improving the lot of over 20,000 widows in India is his widowed mother; and Cherie herself who commits to working with the National Entrepreneurs Network (NEN) to fund, educate and support entrepreneurs in India.

BRIGHT FLAMES AT TWO ENDS

Shabana Azmi's talk on social giving, a range of hard work and dynamic stories from Kiran Mazumdar Shaw, gender neutral policies that Naina Lal Kidwai and Chanda Kochar's corporation have adopted: these are some of the other motivating subjects we listened to.

I'm reminded of two quotations. One is from George Bernard Shaw who said 'Life is no brief candle to me. It is a sort of splendid torch which I have got a hold of for the moment, and I want to make it burn as brightly as possible before handing it on to future generations'. The other is from the Buddha: 'Thousands of candles can be lighted from a single candle, and the life of the candle will not be shortened.' Knowledge never decreases by being shared, I say to myself.

So, new women managers, stay inspired, stay at work, stay connected with role models, simply stay on. India needs you for its progress, and the world needs you for its survival as you naturally understand and nurture people and the planet. Profit of course will follow.

Shreyo bhooyad sakala janaanaam–May good things happen to all people on the planet.

2

TITILLATING THE TASTE BUDS

Developing a Taste for Global Cuisine

The way to all hearts is through the stomach. Global Indians can use this route too. So when you're taking that international trip, go on a culinary tour—you'll most likely end up loving it!

At Global Adjustments our strategic training partner is Syndi Seid, who is a master etiquette consultant in California. Syndi trained Sushmita Sen when she became Miss Universe. Not ready to be trained by anyone less important, I set off to find Syndi and I did. Since then, we have become great friends and co-trainers in Global Indian workshops over the years.

I reproduce here an extract from Syndi's newsletter:

> Some years ago, I attended a backyard barbeque. A man seated at a nearby picnic table was enjoying a meal of ratatouille prepared on a grill. (Until the animated film by the same name was released not so long ago, most people would not have known that ratatouille is a delectable combination of tomatoes, eggplant—better known as brinjal to us Indians—zucchini, onions and herbs native to Italy's Provence region.)
>
> Soon, a woman joined the man at the table and began a conversation by saying, 'Oh, isn't this ratatouille delicious?' The man agreed with much enthusiasm, as he continued to enjoy his meal.
>
> The woman then added, 'I especially like the eggplant.'

> Suddenly, the man came to a screeching halt and asked, 'Eggplant, where's the eggplant?' The woman replied politely, 'Oh, they are the little white squares with the purple skin.'
>
> The man ceased all further eating and said, 'Oh, I hate eggplant!' And with that, he pushed his plate away and didn't eat another bite of that delicious dish.'

Now, I ask you, does that make sense? I didn't think so, which is why I wanted to write about it.

A QUESTION OF LIKES AND DISLIKES

All of us have preconceived notions about what we like and don't like. A question I am regularly asked at my seminars is: 'What should I do if I'm served something I don't like? Do I have to eat it?' Etiquette dictates you must at least taste all the food served to you. To do otherwise would be rude, particularly if you are a guest at someone else's table. Don't insult your host further by saying you don't like it or by drawing attention to the situation. Keep an open mind and try a little of everything served to you. Unless the food item is against your religion, you are allergic to it or it's poisonous, try it; you may like it!

It is said that children develop their eating habits for life before the age of seven. If you are a parent, get beyond your own food preferences. Encourage your children to try new and different foods. Even if at first you must 'make' your child taste something, I promise you, over time your child will develop a palate more accepting of new and different foods.

TAKE A CULINARY CULTURE TOUR

As a bonus, we develop an awareness of the many cultures from which foods originate. And as it becomes easier to travel the world, those who embrace, adapt to and enjoy the cuisines of the world will become the true cosmopolitans of the twenty-first century. Besides, when dining with others for business or social reasons, isn't it always all about whether you like the food and are willing to eat it? 'No! Your focus should be on the friendship and rapport you are building with your friends, family or business associates,' says Syndi.

As Indians travelling the globe, there are meals in different cuisines which actually suit the Indian palate. Or a dash of something added makes a difference to most foods anyway. In Mexican food, the burrito, quesadilla, enchilada or fajita are all similar to our basic paratha or chappatis rolled up with rice, beans, cheese, tomato and then baked. Salsas are like our chutneys and can be added on for additional flavour. The cilantro (coriander, as we know it) used in this cuisine makes us happy as India comes wafting in wherever we smell it!

In Italian food, all pastas with sauces like pomodoro (tomato-based), alfredo (cheese, milk and butter-based), pesto (basil- /tulsi-based) are tasty to Indians. Dry chilly flakes are always available for the asking in Italian restaurants and, when added, seem to take most of us Indians to heaven. Alternatively, ask for or carry your own Tabasco (chilly) sauce.

Falafels from Lebanon are like chickpea vadas; couscous in France is like upuma; udon noodles in Japan are like thick semiya; Chinese wontons or Malay poppiyas are like samosas; and the list goes on. Nasi goreng in Indonesia is a rice dish which can be ordered vegetarian too and their sambhal is red, super-spicy chutney. And, of course, as Syndi says, French ratatouille is delicious for Indians too!

So the next time you travel be open-minded and adventurous, eat what the locals do and find something on the menu that works for you. Let's not go looking all over the world for an Indian restaurant which serves poor Indian food at exorbitant prices. Both will end up giving us indigestion!

Coming to Grips with That Breakfast Order!

Don't allow an elaborate menu card to spoil your appetite. Read on and make an informed choice.

Hungry *kya*, as the pizza advert asks? Well, what are you waiting for? Just order some food to your room when you are on that business trip or conference. Oh! Oh! So many choices . . . and many of them sound peculiar.

Food is a very real problem for many Indians when they go abroad. Western cuisine is very different from what we are used to, and the sheer variety available in each section of a menu card sometimes makes ordering a meal at hotels and restaurants a very daunting task.

ORDER, ORDER!

But I want to talk about ordering a meal in your room to help the business traveller, using the US as an example here. First of all, we need to keep in mind that customizing for individual tastes is a high priority in the West. That's why there are so many choices on offer. You can pick and choose, mix and match. For instance, the menu card may offer a:

1. three-egg omelette with a choice of
   (a) spinach (b) cheddar (c) wild mushrooms and (d) ham
2. two eggs, which can be
   (a) scrambled (b) poached (c) sunnyside up, and (d) over easy

Now what will you make of that?

What's cheddar? some of you may wonder. It's just a type of cheese. And what on earth is an over easy egg? Don't fret; it's another name for what we call 'double fry' here in India.

(Sunnyside up is 'single fry' of course, while poached means the egg is broken into a cup, dropped gently into a pan of boiling water and soft boiled, instead of being fried.) Don't think that you can't go beyond the menu card. If you really like onions in your omelettes, you can ask for them. Most probably, they'll be happy to oblige.

IS IT IN CODE?

You read on, and find that the eggs are accompanied by something called 'hash browns'. That's a tasty mashed potato dish, so give it a try. Then you come to the toast—you find you're being asked to pick from wholewheat, rye, raisin, English muffin and white. Unless you're the adventurous sort, I'd advise you to stick to the white bread: it suits Indians best although wholewheat is better for your health.

There will be a whole list of other choices as well, some of them most exotic-sounding like Cinnamon-Cranberry French Toast. You probably are familiar with the Indian version of this—we call it Bombay Toast here. If you are offered the choice of malted waffle, I'd say go for it; it's sweet but tasty!

You might also come across a range of baked dishes, such as banana walnut bread, pumpkin bread, blueberry muffin, and so on. It's OK to try them out but, remember, they're all sweet to the taste, and many Indians don't like to have something sweet for the first meal of the day.

Old-fashioned oatmeal, cheddar cheese grits and granola are also familiar breakfast items on most foreign menu cards. The first is what we know as oats porridge, the second is something like potato upuma and the last on the list is a cereal.

Even good old coffee and tea come in a variety of choices—you can choose from regular, cream, milk, decaf, skimmed milk or black for the former, and milk, honey, lemon or black for the latter. You'll be safe ordering the regular: milk or skimmed milk coffee and tea with milk.

I've tried to demystify the breakfast menu here; you'll be able to find your way around other menus too if you keep in mind these basic facts—customization is the way they aim to please, and some of the mysterious-sounding items you may already know by some other name. You just need to know what is what.

Here are some tips to get you over that initial nervousness in placing an order in room service.

- *Be ready with your choices* before dialling room service: one person often handles two or three jobs and time is of essence to them.
- However, do feel confident to *ask for clarity* if required.
- We need to know about *tipping practices.* Look at your menu card: Does it mention something about service/ delivery charges per order? If there is, you don't need to tip; a fixed amount has already been added to your bill. If there isn't such a provision, a $2 to $5 tip would be good.
- Finally, most of us are used to being served in bed at home in India but do remember to say *'please' and 'thank you'* even to the waiter/waitress who serves you: our country's image is at stake.

3

IT'S TRADITIONAL!

Traditions That Connect

An understanding of foreign customs and festivals builds stronger cultural ties.

Tradition is an integral part of our lives and sharing it across cultures leads to better relations and builds business. Like a fish immersed in water, we are unaware of the customs we routinely follow. But behind every custom, not only those that we ourselves follow but also those practised by different ethnic and religious groups in our own country and abroad, there are deep underlying meanings.

As India emerges on the world scenario, its borders as well as the minds and hearts of its people are opening up. We in India need to understand the cultural moorings of other nations as well. As you interact with different racial and cultural groups, you will find that you're often asked to explain the significance of a particular custom or festival. It makes sense to understand your own traditions; it will add to your value in the eyes of others. For instance, I explained to an all-American group—at a conference dinner toast I was asked to give for a leader leaving office—that the word 'guru' literally means 'remover of darkness' and that India honours leaders as gurus. After the speech, I had so many people come up to me to say it was most touching to learn this. Equally, take the trouble to understand the customs and traditions of other groups. You'll be surprised to find many parallels and similarities.

I've given below a small selection of defining traditions and festivals of our own country and a few from elsewhere in the world just to give you an idea of what is distinct about us and, also, the common threads.

DISTINCT YET COMMON THREADS

New Year is celebrated all around the world. Mankind is always looking for a new beginning, for another chance, and the New Year represents just that. Different groups and nations may follow different customs and calendars but all the festivities symbolize a fresh start.

Insight for Outsiders:

There's something NEW going on all the time!

In India, different ethnic groups celebrate New Year at different times—there's a Tamil New Year, a Bengali New Year, a Telugu New Year, and so on. But they all follow roughly the same pattern—houses are cleaned and decorated, the household gathers around the family altar and a pooja is conducted to Ganesh, the god of new beginnings. The Goddess of Wealth is also worshipped, and sweets and gifts are handed out.

Bengali tradition requires a mango sapling with a specific number of branches and leaves, symbolizing new life. In Kerala, various objects signifying prosperity and good luck are placed on a tray and children are led to it with their eyes closed, so that the tray will be the first thing they see in the New Year. Elders give other members of the family coins to wish them prosperity. Often, firecrackers are burst to drive away evil spirits.

WELCOMING IN THE NEW YEAR ABROAD

In Japan, when I lived in Saitama, I noticed that the New Year, Oshogatsu, is celebrated on 1 January but Shinto customs are incorporated into the celebrations. A rope of straw is strung across the front of every home, signifying happiness and also to keep out evil. Homes are decorated with evergreens, standing for eternal life. It is a time for the family. Temple bells are rung 108 times to free the people from the 108 earthly desires Buddhism warns against.

A client from Korea, Youngmi Kim, told me how freshly minted coins and other gifts are distributed by the elders on the first day of the lunar year. Sounds familiar?

In China, firecrackers are burst to keep evil spirits at bay, colourful processions are taken out on the streets, homes are cleaned, good luck money is given in red envelopes as the colour signifies joy and homes are decorated with plants thought to be lucky—the Kumquat tree and the peach blossom are the most common.

All over Europe, there's a custom of first-footing, with the first visitor of the New Year considered the harbinger of good fortune.

BRINGING IN THE HARVEST

In agricultural communities like India, the harvest festival is very important and all the rituals are either a thanksgiving for a good crop or an invocation to the gods to ensure a good harvest the next season. In the US, the festival of Thanksgiving, celebrated on the third Thursday of November, also originated as a harvest festival when the first settlers gave thanks to the Almighty for helping their crops flourish in an alien land.

Groundbreaking ceremonies are also more or less universal and though they may differ in detail and ritual, the aim is common. In ancient times, the act of digging the ground for a foundation was thought to hurt Mother Earth and the groundbreaking ceremonies are intended to apologize and make amends. And always, all over the world, now as then, the ceremonies include a prayer for a blessing on the planned construction, and for peace and prosperity for those who live and work in it.

CELEBRATIONS THAT GO WITH A BANG

Moving on, there are so many festivals that are peculiar to one country or another. In India, Diwali is celebrated with gusto not just by Hindus but by all religious groups. Then, there is the Japanese tea ceremony, Halloween in the US, Guy Fawkes Day in the UK, and so on. But even in these country-specific festivals, there's commonality—they all celebrate the victory of good over evil. How strange, you may think. No, not really. It's just one world after all.

So, my advice would be: get to know your own traditions and customs, and get others to participate in them. In the same way, make an effort to understand the cultures of other communities and get involved in them. We will then truly have *Vasudaiva Kutumbakam*—the whole world becoming one family.

Rooted in India and Taking Global Wing

Exercise those Indian traditional muscles, and you're sure to soar high in the world!

I met two extraordinary people recently at a conference in the Indian School of Business. (Run by Wharton in Hyderabad, the campus and education offered at this institute of learning does our country proud.) The first was Charles Savage, a thought leader who spoke on the need for Indian wisdom in the business scenario of the world. 'Are we just going to churn out more and more MBAs?' he asked, seeing a need for the philosophy of the East to balance the effects of consumerism. So he suggested we 'go back to go forward'. His message was that we go back to Indian roots of wisdom to go forward in a sustainable world of developing people and protecting the planet as we continue to make profit.

The other outstanding person was Andy Muffin. He is a speaker in B-schools too and is known as a spiritual coach. Over a coffee after our session he spoke about his own life and what brought him to where he now is—a sought-after visiting faculty in the large schools of the world. As we chatted under a neem tree, this was how his life picture emerged—he had a lovely marriage and a real estate business. He was doing well till greed overtook him. He borrowed too much, built up the business, couldn't sell what he had built and took to drinking. The escape route became a further problem; his wife left him, he was deeply in debt and had to declare bankruptcy. A drive one night ended in a tunnel car crash and broken arms and legs. He had a near-death experience which woke him up to life. He turned to spirituality, rehabilitated himself and became a college professor to teach restraint and common sense along with the engineering he knew well. Today, he explores blending Indian spirituality with his own brand, and inspires students to strengthen the core, the core of our very being so that no external crutch is needed in times of crisis.

Each great nation and race has its own core philosophy to keep it grounded, and when the storms of change and 'progress' come those that hold firmly to these guiding principles remain standing. It's so amazing when you stop to think that so many of the major world religions and philosophies had their origins in the East—from the Middle East to the Far East—Judaism, Islam, Christianity, Hinduism, Buddhism, Jainism,

Sikhism, Confucianism, Shintoism. In India, the spirit of secularism has melded the elements of the religions and philosophies that were born here, almost seamlessly with those that were adopted, making the Indian philosophical fitness equipment even more effective.

The need to strengthen our Indian roots, rely on them for solid grounding and yet be able to soar as high as we can with our global wings is non-negotiable. After all, our GDP is still among the highest in the world. Who can ignore India now or ever again? We will be catapulted into the success field and we will do it in a sustainable way, turning things around for the world, if we hold tight to our core principles.

We are so fortunate in India to be surrounded by core strengthening gadgets.

THE DHARMA REEBOK BALL

Sanatana dharma or eternal values is the original name of Hinduism, as we know. Dharma can be explained as a set of rules of behaviour laid down by the Hindu scriptures, which makes sure we stay on the path of righteousness. It's a sort of fusion of moral laws and spiritual discipline, and when you keep to these codes you're observing natural universal laws which will keep you fulfilled. In simpler terms, it means doing what is right, not merely for yourself but in the larger contexts of the family, the society, the country, the world and the universe itself. It means that all your decisions have to be taken with reference to the greater good. Like balancing on the big rubber Reebok ball and feeling wobbly at first while you do core exercises in a gym, it is practice that keeps you fit.

THE PANCHA BHOOTA ABS WORKOUT BAR

As an extension of these universal laws, Indian philosophy is rooted in a Single Reality, which, however, manifests in many forms, each of which is deserving of reverence. The Hindu scriptures teach that there are five basic elements—wind, water, fire, earth and space—and all facets of creation are combinations of these. In fact, our bodies are also a product of the same five—wind is in the form of our breath; water, we see as tears or sweat; fire in the stomach contributes to digestion; the body remains at 98.6 degrees F normally; earth is there as potassium, sodium and minerals; and of course the body occupies space (to reduce the space occupied we go to the gym these days). Leading our lives in harmony with the five elements respects nature and reduces our own lofty ego, much like crunching up towards an abs workout bar handle: the pain is a 'nice' pain as it leads to a midsection getting reduced to a six-pack eventually!

THE SHANTI GRIPPER

Hinduism, like other world religions, recognizes peace as the absolute objective of life. Indian philosophy teaches us that peace is within each one of us and, to find it, thought-provoking chants are recommended. Prayers in Hinduism often end with the chanting of the words 'Om Shanti' thrice—peace from natural disasters, people around you and your inner thoughts. It is based on the belief that whatever is said thrice comes true. (Incidentally, this belief in the power of three is shared by other major religions. Christian prayer services end with the word 'Amen', a solemn statement which means 'Before God I want it to be so', repeated thrice. In the Islamic tradition also, the thrice-repeated word is very potent.)

To get back to the Shanti Gripper—like the gadget that you grip and release often to strengthen your wrist and fist, use chanting, prayer, meditation and mind strengthening grippers often to get a 'grip on life'. The pressures and conflicts of the commercial world become more manageable.

THE KARMA ELLIPTICAL MACHINE

Again, ancient Indian philosophy dictates that our actions set off a cycle of cause and effect. It isn't only our deeds that produce karma, according to Indian sages, it is also our thoughts, our words and the things others do under our orders. Indian philosophy says that the effects of karma influence our present, and also impact our past and future. So then let us practise weighing our thoughts, words and deeds in order to shape a better today and a brighter tomorrow.

What goes around comes around, much like the EFX machine at the gym which effectively burns calories as we cyclically step up and down on it. Increasing resistance is key in both the machine and in performing 'right' actions.

THE MAHA YAGNA CIRCUIT TRAINING

We are expected like circuit training to do different kinds of exercises for different parts of our body in a gym, to serve different aspects of the world for overall good. Yagna is worship of the different elements that make up Creation and Nature, reminding us to put back what we take out, so that the balance of the universe isn't disturbed. This is vital to harmonious living and a daily prescribed act in Hinduism of revering five elements—god, scriptures, forefathers, humans, and the plant and animal kingdom. You could do your bit by prayer (to show reverence to God), funding spiritual education institutions (to revere scriptures), contributing to geriatric care (to revere forefathers), being kind to your fellow workers (for human contribution), and contributing to green causes (for plants and animals).

Charles and Andy said India has it all; we can soar high, if we also stay rooted in our own philosophy.

PUT IN A NUTSHELL

'Plurality makes life wonderful, it is the inherent oneness that makes life meaningful.'

—Swami Parmarthananda

To be an effective cross-cultural person simply remember the word CARE—C is Clarity in communication; A is Adapting to the other's ways; R is Respect for differences; and E is Empathy or being in their shoes. If you also CARE truly, then cross-cultural understanding will come naturally. No one teaches us this at B-school or even A-school. So thank you for taking the time to learn it additionally today.

As we proceed on the never-ending journey of learning in life, we come to realize that the more we practise what we learn, the better it will come to us naturally. What will matter is not just the goal but the footsteps we take to reach it. We can leap, stumble, fall, pick ourselves up and make this global business. Or we can measure our steps and chart our own path to reach it feeling prepared and victorious through it all.

Build bridges so that commerce can go on easily both ways. As the world becomes more and more of a global village, standardization becomes increasingly important, especially in matters of communication. In the business of being a Global Indian, we need to give up idiosyncrasies and go with what is universally practised——a lesson I learnt when I tried to spell my name while reconfirming a reservation in the US over the phone. 'MANIAN', I said—'M as in Monkey, A as in Ahmedabad, N as in Nagpur, I as in Ink, A as in Ahmedabad again and N as in

Nasik.' 'Lady, I was less confused before you started,' the American replied! I now use the international spelling code—'A as in Alpha, B as in Bravo . . .'

We have discussed here how best to speak, in person or via gadgets, while getting on with others. We have measured actions and reactions to take to be in sync with people whose mindset is different from ours. We can network to leave an impression, make a meeting efficient, and make friends for life by speaking their language; we can make business happen through attention to little details. We have taken a walk through international etiquette in a business setting, and also seen how the West can help us improve on our manners and, so, win and keep friends.

At the end of the day, it's all about give and take: in a marriage, in a cultural relationship or even in life. Build on your strengths, know your intrinsic values and become a master at any game you choose. Most important of all, know yourself—your culture, your traditions and your values. Be proud of these, and share the Best of India with the rest of the globe. Together, we can make the world a better place!

Hello India, World calling; are you ready?
Be a Global Indian.

ETIQUETTE QUIZ

Here's a fun quiz for you on etiquette in today's Global Indian or global citizen business world.

1. During a business meet/meal, is it permissible to place my cellphone on the table?

   (a) Always.
   (b) Never.
   (c) Only when I am expecting a call.

The correct answer is (b).

(Alas, this life of the ubiquitous cellphone! It follows us everywhere as flushing noises have proven!) Nothing should be placed on the table that is not directly related to the meeting or meal itself (your glasses, a handkerchief or tissue paper, a cellphone and a Blackberry, a purse, keys . . . nothing at all). If at a business meet/meal, the business at hand should be the most important conversation, not an incoming call. If dining/meeting one-on-one, the person 'in person' should receive your full attention. If expecting an urgent call, let your party know in advance that you may need to be excused, keep your phone in your pocket or on your lap—out of sight in the 'Vibrate' mode. Take the call away from the table and keep it as brief as possible. Women can keep their handbags by their feet or behind their backs, leaning lightly against it, thus sitting upright on the chair.

2. When is it OK to discuss client business on a cellphone in a semi-private area?

(a) Anytime.
(b) Only when it is urgent.
(c) Email if it is a private address. Cellphone if not many people are around.
(d) Never.

The correct answer is (d).

Despite the fact that most people do not seem to distinguish between personal and private conversations on their cellphones, client business should never be discussed if 'anyone' is around and certainly not on elevators or in corridors, stores, restaurants, food courts or other public areas, even if you don't know anyone around you. As an exception, Official Urgent Cell conversations need to be conducted with a hand cupped over the microphone briefly and quietly.

3. When you are finished eating, your napkin should be
   (a) dropped to the ground as you rise from the chair.
   (b) folded loosely and placed on the left side of the plate.
   (c) folded loosely and placed at the centre of the plate.
   (d) placed on the seat of your chair.

The correct answer is (b).

It should be folded loosely and placed on the left side of your plate. Your napkin should be placed on your chair if you temporarily leave the table. Don't forget to push your chair in. Use the fork with your left hand and the knife, with your right; avoid making chomping noises and you will be a good diner.

4. Gift-giving is discouraged or limited by many US/ European and multinational companies. A gracious written note is always appropriate and acceptable.

(a) True.
(b) False.

The correct answer is (a).

If you do give a gift, it should not appear to be a bribe. An invitation for a meal or a modest gift is usually acceptable.

5. When wearing name tags, the best place to put my name tag is below my left shoulder area.
   (a) True.
   (b) False.

The correct answer is (b).

Ideally, you should place your name tag below your right shoulder because during the handshake (using your right hand), the other person's eyes naturally follow your right arm up to your head to make eye contact, allowing time to slip another look on the way up that same arm at the name tag, instead of having to look over to the other shoulder to see a name tag on the left side.

6. For email introductions, what is an appropriate way to start off?
   (a) I am happy to introduce myself, Mr Ram Sharma, VP, XYZ Company.
   (b) Allow me to introduce myself. I am Ram Sharma, VP, XYZ Company.

The correct answer is (b).

You are happy to introduce someone to someone else and you seek permission to introduce yourself: that is great business etiquette. Also you never put a 'Mr' or 'Ms' before your own name.

7. When you are introducing your colleague Tom Cruise on email do you say
   (a) my manager, Tom Cruise.
   (b) Tom Cruise, relocation manager at Global Adjustments.
   (c) Tom Cruise, our relocation manager.

The correct answer is (b).

The idea is to be as efficient and professional and this option states the full name, title and company in that order.

If you need to convey that you report to this person, it is fine to add: 'I have escalated or included Tom Cruise, relocation manager, Global Adjustments, for further clarity on the matter as he is the team lead on this project or as I work for his team and he can advise you best.' (c) is also an acceptable response; (a) is least favourable as it stresses personal relation over professional role.

8. When I have a cold, and I am in a meeting, it is most appropriate to
   (a) sniffle and make sounds with my nose, throat or other such organ, to prevent flow of mucous
   (b) blow into a tissue and throw the tissue in the trash.
   (c) blow into a tissue and keep the tissue in my pocket.
   (d) excuse myself, blow my nose hard, throw the tissue away, wash my hands and come back to the meeting, then use a tissue to wipe my nose and make sure I don't touch anyone or anything else for the rest of the meeting, coughing or sneezing into the crook of my elbow.

The correct answer is (b).

Sneezing into the crook of the elbow prevents the spread of germs better; sniffles throughout a meeting are very annoying to the other people; using a tissue and handling others after is not acceptable as it spreads germs. It is best to say I won't shake hands as I have a cold. Clear your nose, wash your hands and then continue the meeting.

9. In India, the sound *Pcch* with teeth closed and lips slightly open is a sound that means understanding or agreement, clicking the tongue on the roof of the mouth way at the back to make a 'click' sound means 'no' and rounding of the mouth with small frequent string of sounds 'ch ch ch ch' shows sympathy or care. It's OK to use these in speech and a Westerner needs to understand Indian ways.
   (a) True.
   (b) False.

The correct answer is (b).

These sounds are repetitive and Western people don't understand what exactly they mean. It makes us sound less professional in a dialogue to suddenly have lips and tongue clicking away, so they are habits best dropped. Replacing these sounds with 'I do understand', 'Not really' or 'not yet, I am afraid' are all much more sophisticated communication tools and will take you on the path from being a mediocre to a magnificent professional.

10. For internal and external emails, which is the most suitable salutation to be used?
    (a) Hi.
    (b) Dear . . . (name).
    (c) None.
    (d) Name.

The correct answer is (b).

It is the best response as it is courteous and personalized; (d) is also okay and speaks to their heart; (c) and (a) are always too informal unless you address the person by name in the first sentence somewhere. Having one form for all communication makes you an expert at business writing and shows that you are treating your external and internal customers with the same courtesy and respect that you appreciate yourself.

Office Etiquette: Rate Yourself Game

For every 'yes' give yourself 10 points; for every partial 'yes' give 5.

If you scored more than 100, you have good office manners. Keep at it.

If you scored less than 50, you need to learn office manners. Work harder.

If you were in between, you need to continue in your awareness.

1. I keep personal phone calls to a minimum in length and frequency at work.
2. I take friendly breaks of three to five minutes with colleagues and come back to my concentrated job.
3. I take 15 + minute breaks to discuss non-work related issues with colleagues.
4. When I speak to co-workers I wouldn't be afraid if I was overheard.
5. I never use MSN messenger or personal emails at work without prior permission.
6. I always greet everyone including office helpers with a smile and a greeting.
7. I thank co-workers and use please for all requests.
8. I give feedback in writing or through email regularly.

9. I use a diary to carry forward jobs and to track my time as others depend on me.
10. I don't ask others to fetch or carry or do other errands for me that I can do myself.
11. I come prepared for meetings and participate productively.
12. I am never/rarely late (to work, to meetings, to appointments).

ACKNOWLEDGEMENTS

I would like to thank the following people who contributed in so many ways to making *Upworldly Mobile* a reality:

Swami Parmarthananda, for putting so many ideas into my head about how to listen with respect and reply without rancour, to get on with the world.

Dr Sashi Tharoor, for so generously giving his time and insights to write the Foreword for this book.

All the leaders and trainers who allowed me to quote them in the book.

Susan Philip, my reliable, talented and organized editorial coordinator, without whom the book could not have seen the light of day.

Praveena Shivram, for suggesting the clever twist in the title.

Pascal Reynand, my talented photo artist of Vietnamese-French origin who captured the spirit of the book in the cover design.

The Penguin team—Heather, Udayan, Ankita and others—for having seen the book through.

My sister, Kamini, who not only cheered for me but also contributed to my global perspective.

My bright and bubbly team at Global Adjustments, for having been with me at every step of my *Upworldly Mobile* venture.

My daughter Rohini, son Varun and husband Manian for encouraging me always in all I do.

And last, but by no means least, the thousands of clients at Venture Global Adjustments who, over a decade and a half, made me and my team pay more attention to India, and gain new insights into this magnificent country of ours. Thank you for helping us know ourselves, as that was the first step to know you.

I gratefully acknowledge you all.